Teaching Without Tears

Teaching Without Tears

Your First Year in the Secondary School

by Jenny Gray

Norte del Rio High School, Sacramento, California

Consultant: *James R. Erickson*, Principal,
Norte del Rio High School, Sacramento, California

Drawings by *Robert Haydock*

FEARON PUBLISHERS *fp* **Palo Alto, Calif.**

Preface

"Teacher training" is a misnomer. Today's teacher candidate in most American colleges and universities receives a thorough indoctrination in the philosophy and theory of education; he learns to evaluate the accomplishments and shortcomings of the American secondary school; he learns to design and conduct educational research projects. But, typically, he won't emerge from his teacher training course any wiser than he entered it as far as the everyday functions, tools, and booby traps of his trade are concerned. What will he *do* all day long? He won't know, exactly; and his fumblings will become a source of humiliation to himself, exasperation to his co-workers, and chaos to his hapless students.

It's true he will get his toes damp (not really wet) in his practice teaching experience. But something beyond this token baptismal sprinkling is required to convert college seniors, no matter how dedicated, into competent practitioners of the instructional arts in today's secondary schools. Although the material contained in this book moves in the direction of meeting this need, the reader should be cautioned against viewing it as a pedagogical panacea to the problem of the well-educated but poorly-trained teacher.

In the first place, this is a cookbook (no apology offered); and, like all cookbooks, its usefulness will be limited. A recipe may tell you to break an egg into the batter, but not what to do should the egg turn out to be rotten. More important, there are other educators who are undoubtedly better qualified than I to write a book of this kind, but so far they haven't. Until such time as their consciences goad them into coming forward to do their duty, I find myself operating as a self-appointed oracle. It is only fair, therefore, that the reader be advised of the source of the oracular preachments he will find in the pages to come.

First, I drew on a ten-year accumulation of shoptalk with teacher colleagues, both "new" and "old," in Arkansas, Indiana, Arizona, and California. Elementary school teachers,

as well as junior and senior high school teachers, are repre-
sented, as are teachers in the antipoverty and manpower
training schools and from adult education programs.

Second, I am indebted for the off-the-cuff accounts of
experiences and the value judgments of a number of supervisors and principals, most notably my present principal,
James Erickson.

Third, there is my own 11,000 hours in the classroom and
2,000 hours of service with teacher organizations, in-service
training programs, student clubs, and so on. Mention should
also be made of a three-year period of writing, testing, researching, and classroom teaching with programmed instruction and educational systems. The ideas implicit in both
programming and educational systems have made a singular
impact on teaching practice generally. Many suggestions
throughout *Teaching Without Tears* will illustrate that they
have affected my teaching particularly.

My own teacher training was not much help in preparing
this book. Although I frequently consulted textbooks and old
class notes, it was to decide what material should be left out,
not to check up on material I intended to put in. If an item
of information was covered in the textbooks—at least in *my*
textbooks—I felt there was nothing to be gained by covering
it again; so, for the most part, I didn't. There are a few
exceptions. Test construction is one, for in many states
teachers enter employment before they have completed requirements for a general credential and may not have been
exposed to training in tests and measurements.

Teaching Without Tears will have been written in vain if
it doesn't start a few good arguments. The people who should
have written this book but didn't, will disagree with many
of the assumptions made and positions taken. Good! I'm
flexible; maybe they'll change *my* mind. There's only one
point I feel so strongly about that I'd refuse to budge an inch:
The classroom and what goes on in it is tremendously important to all of us—so important that it deserves vastly
more attention than it's getting.

JENNY GRAY

Contents

one

Welcome to the Club

Months, weeks, or, because the world of education moves
quickly nowadays, a few hours ago, you were offered your
first teaching position and accepted it. Lucky you! From an
historical point of view, you couldn't have happened along
in a better time or place. Never before has a nation exhibited
such interest in its public schools or been so willing to part
with hard cash to improve them.

Education is in the process of becoming the biggest business
in the land. In doing so, it has inevitably attracted the interest of big industry. Technological innovations now in the
process of development will find their way into nearly all
of the nation's schools within the next ten years—your first
years in the classroom—and into schools in the rest of the
world for the next hundred years. You, yourself, will pioneer
in the use of many of these innovations.

It will be a thrilling and rewarding time, but not necessarily
an easy one. Pioneers run into difficulties. The man who, at
sixty-five, has the satisfaction of boasting, "Our family owned

I

the first automobile in town," can also tell you about the time the family was without transportation for two weeks while his father tried unsuccessfully to patch a tire. In your turn, you will be able to say proudly that yours was the first school in the county to schedule and report grades by computer. But you may also recount to your grandchildren how you flunked all your students one semester because you misunderstood instructions for bubbling your class cards for the computer.

These adventures will come in due time. At the moment, the greatest adventure of all, your first year of teaching, awaits you. With the proper planning, it can be one of the most thrilling years of your life.

Meet Your Principal

After you have signed your contract, go to your school for a private conference with your principal as soon as possible. He will show you your classroom and see that keys are issued so you can come and go as you like. He will talk to you about school philosophy, go over the curriculum related to your teaching assignment, and review daily routine as it affects your particular schedule. During the discussion, the principal will give you some basic understanding of how he deals with his faculty. He will explain teacher ratings and faculty meetings.

The principal will inform you about terms commonly used in the school. Do they call it "homeroom," "division," or "registration" period? Is it "college prep," "academic," or "honors" track? The principal will explain how materials, supplies, and audio-visual equipment are obtained. He will indicate how deeply he expects you to become involved in extracurricular activities. He will discuss both district and school policy concerning classroom discipline.

The principal can also give you advice about other things. He can steer you away from that groovy apartment smack in the middle of the town's red-light district, for example.

Looking for a roommate? He can make a phone call or two and line up some people for you to talk to. He may send you to the district office to fill out forms for withholding federal and state taxes and to sign up for insurance plans offered by the district. Attending to these details early takes the pressure off you later on.

Most important of all, the principal will give you your copy of the teachers' handbook. This literary treasure, usually mimeographed and stapled together, comprises the school's operation and procedures manual, calendar, Bible, and helpful household hints, all packed together in one volume. Nothing will be as valuable the first week of school as this handbook. Underline and make marginal notes to your heart's content; it's yours. Every hour spent studying its contents will avoid three hours of wasted time later on, when you can least afford to squander it.

On your initial visit to the school, you may meet your department head, the secretaries (good people to know), and perhaps a few of your new colleagues. If circumstances permit, take time to get to know these people. You will be asking them a lot of questions.

Your Preschool Homework

After you have said good-by to your principal at the end of your first conference, gather together the goodies he has turned over to you and go home and study as you have never studied before.

First, try to get an over-all picture of what duties the teacher—any teacher—in your school is expected to perform and how he is expected to go about performing them. Be sure you understand how the schedule works; the lunch periods may be tricky. Make a list of your responsibilities as homeroom teacher. In most schools, homeroom is a housekeeping period where lockers are assigned, textbooks are checked out to students for the year, accident insurance cards are filled out for the school clinic, and so on. Slip-ups in numbering and irregularities in alphabetical order may seem inconsequential details at the time, but they may be with you all year and compound your clerical difficulties from week to week. Try to get it right the first time.

Once the homeroom operation is clear to you, take a moment to consider your teaching assignment. A one-preparation teaching load is generally considered tops. If you have only one lesson plan to worry about, you'll have time to make that one plan a good one. You'll be able to track down the supplementary material you need, type up the spirit duplicator masters, prepare the charts, and so on. But a one-preparation assignment isn't always as appetizing as it appears on the surface. For one thing, five classes in ninth-grade science, for example, won't be all that much alike. Some sections will learn faster than others. Also, assemblies and pep rallies will throw one or two classes behind.

The fact that the classes themselves aren't synchronized presents no problem, but complications arise when you finish the unit and give the test on different days. Your test scores will rise from day to day as information about the test items gets around among your other students. Students in the last section to take the test will have picked the brains of students from earlier sections and will, therefore, have an unfair advantage. To an extent, you can control this by placing all scores on the same curve and pointing out to your first-period students how they scuttle themselves by squealing to the last-period students, but you won't get rid of the problem entirely.

Another fly in the one-preparation ointment is that teaching the same lesson plan over and over can be tiresome. If you're planning to give the same test to each class, you must obviously say and do the same things with each class, bring out the same points when you go over the homework assignment, and provide the same commentary on the text. Month after month of going through four carbon copies of the same class can give you a minor hang-up. You might find yourself in a worse fix than the first-grade teacher with the flat tire. It won't be, "Oh, oh, oh; look, look, look; damn, damn, damn"; it will be "Oh, oh, oh, oh oh; look, look, look, look, look; damn, damn, damn, damn, *damn*!!!"

The most vicious assignment possible is at the other extreme, to have five different preparations—for example, one tenth-grade basic English, one twelfth-grade college prep English, one twelfth-grade business English, one first-year French, and one second-year French. Administrators avoid such assignments, because they realize it means a year of sloppy teaching; it isn't humanly possible to do a decent job with such a nightmare of subjects and students to teach. Yet, sometimes there are circumstances an administrator can't control. He may have staffed his school for 1,500 students, and on opening day 1,700 show up. When this happens,

he must abandon arrangements for what he knows to be good education and do what he can with the personnel available. The situation becomes even worse when he must hand this difficult assignment, not to an experienced teacher, but to a hired-at-the-last-minute tyro already suffering from first-year jitters. (A good reason for getting your teaching job lined up early. The last hired get the roughest assignments.) If there is a shortage of classrooms as well, this teacher will "float," meeting his first-period students in this classroom, second-period students in that classroom, upstairs, downstairs, east wing, west wing, carrying his books and supplies with him as he goes.

Needless to say, the fundamental problem for such a teacher isn't instruction at all; it is survival. He must cut out nonessentials and get all the help he can from other teachers, supervisors, and the school's clerical staff, all of whom will be aware of his plight. He will have all the help he needs if he asks for it. Most important of all, he should indulge in a perspicacious amount of good-natured bellyaching to the proper authorities ("proper" being the ones he can get to listen) to make certain he gets a fair shake his second year.

Quo Vadis?

Just as experienced playwrights often write the last act first, many experienced teachers revise last year's final exam, or compose a new one from the course of study, as the year's first item of business. With this statement of teaching goals written down and available as a guide for teaching strategy throughout the year, they are ready to construct their unit tests, units, and daily lesson plans in a sensible way.

You may, if you wish, borrow a final examination from your department head or from a colleague with the same teaching assignments as yours, and use it as a guide for your year's teaching. It wouldn't be a good idea to construct your own final examination before you've acquired some experience in the classroom. You may be forced to work out your lesson plans directly from the course of study your first year, but construct your first-year final exams with permanent use in mind.

Before school starts is the time to make up tentative lesson plans for your first week. Don't work out final details or type up spirit duplicator masters for instructional material until you have gone over the plans with your department head. He will know whether your level of difficulty is too high or too low for the students who have been assigned to you, whether the film you have scheduled is likely to be available, and whether there is enough equipment to go around.

Don't plan to do anything but get acquainted the first day. You will be too busy with other things to try anything serious in the way of instruction.

Go through your lesson plan book and write in assemblies, rallies, and school holidays in pencil on the dates on which they will take place. You will find these in your teachers' handbook (look in the Index under "Calendar"). There may be changes, so fill them in your lesson plan book only up to Thanksgiving.

From the course of study, try to make a tentative decision as to what you'd like to cover the first semester and what in the second. Read your textbooks. (Yes, that's right; read your textbooks.) Make marginal notes in pencil as ideas come to you for lesson plans. How does the textbook material tie in with the course of study? Make pencil notes on the table of contents or in the text itself about what to include and what to omit. Does the course of study call for instruction in areas for which you seem to have no material at all? Write yourself a reminder to ask your department head about it.

Your Classroom

Take an afternoon off from your study session to go back to school for a look at the room where you will teach. It will be your job to turn your classroom into an educational "home" for your students. If you don't have a knack for beautification but your wife does, bring her along.

If you are in an old building, there are certain things to watch out for. That yellowed picture of Horace Mann you want to take down is undoubtedly hiding a rectangle of pale wall. Take Horace Mann down, but be sure your new photograph will cover the pale spot on the wall. Don't throw away those slender, two-foot lengths of wood. They are there to hold the windows in place when you open them—so they won't come crashing down and break the glass in the panes.

Go slow about discarding any strange wands, hooks, knobs, or screws you find in the room. Your predecessor may have scrounged for months to obtain these items, and he may have left them for you with tenderness in his heart. They are for something—to open the transom, turn on the radiator, or unlock the steel file.

If you have a cracked window, notify the principal right away, in writing, so he'll have a note to route to the custodian. Give your name, room number, and window(s) identification. Do the same for damaged desks or broken shelving. No, it may not all be fixed before the students arrive for the first day of school; but send the note anyway. Your chances of getting something done about it now, before the other teachers arrive and send in their notes, are better than they'll ever be.

How will you black out your room to show films? Are there shades? *Whole* ones? Masking tape makes excellent patching material if the shades are frayed. If you discover you cannot show films in your classroom but must share a viewing room with several other teachers, it's better to find out ahead of time so you can take account of it in your lesson planning.

You may decide to do a bit of painting—not the room, of course, but perhaps a reading table or a set of shelves. Check with your department head or principal first. Don't ask unless you really intend to do it. You'll get the green light if the building is five years old or more.

Want an extra table in your room? Study carrels? A magazine rack? Talk to your department head. Equipment inventories are sometimes kept on a departmental basis and sometimes on a building-wide basis. You'll need to find out who is the man to see in your school.

Sometimes furniture swaps are worked out between teachers themselves: "I'll trade you the five lab chairs I don't need for your extra specimen case." But wait to see how many students show up before doing anything about student desks.

Don't expect to get everything you feel you need by the end of the first week or the first month—or even the first year if it's an item that costs fifty dollars or more. Seniority plays a big part in who gets what, and for a good reason. What has happened the longest is most likely to keep on happening. It makes sense for the district to invest money in a teacher who has taught the same subject in the same room for four years; he will probably be open for business at the same lemonade stand for quite a while yet. On the other hand, a first-year teacher might get married and quit, or transfer. Who knows?

If your building is new, you're in luck. There will be less difficulty in making your classroom look cheerful and livable. Plastic sprays of ivy and philodendron, paper flowers, and dried grasses all make attractive and durable decorations. If your bulletin board stumps you, get yourself a book of bulletin board ideas. You'll probably find one in the library's collection of teachers' professional books.

Set off a bulletin board area no smaller than 2′ x 3′ for posting school notices. You will need another area about the same size on the chalkboard (not the bulletin board) for present, past, and future homework assignments. You might want to decorate your assignment board with colored chalk, which you can get from the art teacher.

Caution: Use masking tape for putting pictures on your chalkboard. The gummed backing from cellophane tape is almost impossible to remove. Instead of washing your chalkboard, ask the custodian for the special cleaner to be used on it. Water will warp it. If you can't get the special cleaner, work on it with a barely-damp sponge and a clean, dry cloth.

Before you drive nails into your walls for pictures, ask someone. There may be a certain kind of nail you should use.

You can get a fresh desk blotter from the office at the same time you get your paper clips, rubber bands, ruler, stapler, and pads of hall passes and absence slips. While you're getting these things, ask if there are book ends and letter trays available for issue to teachers. You'll need a set of book ends to organize the top of your desk, and a double set of letter trays is a necessity for incoming (to be graded) and outgoing (graded, ready to return to students) reports, exercises, and themes.

If you do not have one at home and are not issued one, buy yourself a desk calendar with a separate sheet for each day. It is on this calendar that you will remind yourself when you are to supervise the football game, when the next faculty meeting is scheduled, and so on.

Female teachers only: How's the view from the student side when you are seated at your desk? If you have one of those see-through jobs, get the custodian to bring you a desk with a back to it. There'll be days when you'll want to adjust your girdle, and that's nobody's business but yours.

Examine your chair and desk for splinters or nails that might snag your clothing; sand them down or pound them in. (Ladies can make do with an emery board and a high-heeled shoe.) Chair squeak? Grease it. Is it too high or too low? Adjust the knobs underneath until it's the right height. Your desk and chair will be your work area thirty-five hours a week for the next nine months. Fix them and forget it.

District Orientation

When you signed your contract, you were given a mimeographed sheet of information about your new school district. Somewhere on that sheet may be found the date and time you must report for regular staff meetings that all teachers will attend. The meetings you're especially interested in, however, are the new-teacher orientation meetings, which will be scheduled a day or two prior to the regular ones.

After your classroom has been prepared to your satisfaction, or nearly so, you will want to glance over your teachers' handbook once more. If you have done your homework thoroughly, the scheduled new-teacher orientation will make sense to you. You'll be able to ask intelligent questions and know what to do with the answers you receive.

You will be ill at ease when you arrive for this first orientation meeting, but you shouldn't be. The people in charge will be charming, helpful, and not in the least forbidding. The meeting will probably start on time, so get there! If it turns out you're the one who's early and the school people are running late, strike up conversations with the other new teachers gathered about. You'll be seeing them all again later.

When it comes to the agenda, orientation meetings usually start at the top and work down. By that I mean they will consider matters of concern to the entire district first, then proceed to the individual school level, and finish in your own department.

There's often an exhilarating, "sick-'em-tiger" atmosphere about these meetings, and you may emerge feeling so oriented you're ready to lick your weight in chalkboard erasers. Not

until much later will you discover that few people in your
district are satisfied with the way new-teacher orientation is
handled, least of all the administrators. The difficulty isn't
in planning and conducting good orientation programs; most
of them are excellent. The problem is that there are so many
different kinds of "new teachers."

The range of individual differences among new staff members is even wider than the range among the students who
are to be served by them. At your meeting, for example, you
may sit beside a nurse with five years experience in a clinic
who is taking her first job in a school. In front of you may
be a shop teacher who left this same district three years ago
to take a job in industry and is now returning. Beside him
may be a basketball coach who has transferred from a school
district a thousand miles away, where he worked for eight
years. Behind you may be a speech therapist fresh from his
university training, with no school experience at all. And so
it goes. But all these people will have things they need to
learn about the district and its relationship to its staff
members.

Much of the information given to this mixed bag of new,
not so new, and downright old personnel will be tossed out
as a sort of refresher course. This is fine for the majority of
the group, who will already be familiar with schools in
general. But a refresher course won't be enough for the
honest-to-Pete, mint-green new teachers like you, which is
why you went to visit your principal early. The *real* new
teachers need a head start.

Your first scheduled orientation session will be a district
affair. You'll meet the superintendent, who will welcome his
new teachers and perhaps escort them on a bus tour of the
schools in the district. The serious business of your district
orientation will be teacher certification and matters having
to do with your paycheck.

You do know by now that certification is your responsibility. Health clearance is also your responsibility. You will
need chest X-rays and a physical examination at the time
you apply for your certificate or before you go to work. By

the time you have signed a contract and the end of August has arrived, it is assumed that you have obtained health clearance and that your certificate is in your possession or is in the last stages of processing. Almost everywhere, a teacher must produce proof of good health and of proper certification before the district can legally issue the teacher's first pay voucher. In every school in which you'll ever teach, there will be at least one legend of some trouble-prone beginner who ran afoul of the bureaucrats and lived in a sixth-floor walk-up on cereal and water for two months before the first paychecks came through.

This brings us to the matter of your paycheck and how it's processed before you get it. These points may be explained to you at your district orientation meeting; but if they aren't, you need to know what's ahead so you can make plans for a fall and winter budget.

If you've ever been on anyone's payroll before, anywhere, you already realize that there is a certain amount of shrinkage that takes place between your scheduled rate of pay and the amount you actually deposit in your account at the bank on payday.

First, you must understand how your district happened to offer you the salary it did. Someplace in that stack of paper you have accumulated is a salary scale for your district. Although it's true no two districts have the same scale, the way they're set up tends to follow a pattern. Across the top of the salary scale page, reading from left to right, will be column headings representing degrees of academic preparation: A.B., A.B. plus 15 hours, A.B. plus 30 hours, A.B. plus master's, and so on. There will be fine points you may not understand. You are expected to, and you should talk to your principal if the amount on your contract doesn't seem to jibe with the salary scale. There may be additional questions you need answered before you can understand how the scale was interpreted in arriving at your contract figure; for example: A.B. plus what kind of hours? Graduate hours only? Education hours only? Quarters or tri-mester hours? Hours from certain institutions only? Hours earned within the last five years?

Down the left side of the salary scale will be steps representing years of experience. Suppose you taught a half-year or taught in summer school only? What credit are you given for teaching in another district? Thrash all this out with your principal. But be sure you understand how the district happened to place you on the pay scale where it did.

So much for the amount on the salary scale you are being paid. How about deductions? The biggest deduction will be federal income tax. For withholding federal income tax, all employers have fixed schedules that they are required by law to follow. You may, if you wish, phone the payroll department in your district and find out to the penny what this amount will be in your case; or you may consult the tax table in the Internal Revenue Service tax form book that comes to you in the mail every January and figure it out yourself. Then there is your state or city income tax deduction, if there is one. Social security, which will appear on your pay voucher as FICA (Federal Insurance Compensation Act), is 4.4 per cent of your gross salary up to a total of $290.40. The amount taken out for retirement, like state and city income tax, will vary according to state law governing this deduction. Most states' teacher retirement laws have some provision for a matching of your deductions by the district in which you work. Seldom will the percentage be much higher than 7 per cent for men and slightly more for women (because they live longer).

Having subtracted the deductions you will definitely have,

divide your remaining salary by twelve (months) and, give or take fifteen dollars, that's your take-home pay. You may also choose to have the district deduct payments for insurance, credit union obligations, dues for professional organizations, or other payments from your paycheck before you get it.

That's all? Not quite. Let's consider how you're going to receive your salary. If you let matters take their course, you will most probably be paid over the nine-month school period, either every two weeks or once a month. If so, think twice before you spend it all. It isn't wise to spend your salary as fast as you earn it during the school year with the happy notion you might get a job in the summer months when no school money is coming in. Many a teacher ruefully discovers the job he "might" get over the summer never materializes, and he begins to feel the pinch about July 4th. By the end of September, when the next paycheck is due, it won't matter if the local utility company has cut off his electricity, because there wasn't anything in the refrigerator to keep cold anyway.

There are a number of ways you can provide for money to live on over the summer. By far the soundest is to make arrangements at the credit union to have about 25 per cent of your net (not gross) salary deducted every payday. Through the fall and winter months, while your deposits are building up at the credit union, you will be receiving interest. Through the summer, you withdraw amounts (shares) as you need them to live on. Not so good is to perform this operation in reverse—borrow money from the credit union during the summer as you need it and pay it back, with interest, during the following school year. Before the credit union people will let you do this, you will have to show them you have a contract for the following year, naturally; and you will probably have to put up some collateral as well.

Many districts offer their teachers the option of nine-month or twelve-month pay plans. If you elect to receive your money over a twelve-month period, you receive no interest on your withheld summer money. In rare instances, there will be districts where the choice isn't left up to you at all. Your contract will simply read that you are to be paid in twelve equal installments (no interest).

I have talked about the teachers' credit union without actually explaining what it is. It is a kind of co-operative savings and loan association run by and for school personnel. It may be organized by the teachers in one district only, or by the personnel from several districts in a city or county. It is operated under a federal credit union law, which places it under federal scrutiny and control; in other words, no one is likely to abscond with money you invest there. New teachers can join by opening an account with a minimum deposit, usually five dollars.

The credit union can lend you money at a lower rate of interest than comparable institutions in your area, primarily because it has almost no bad loans or collection problems. Payments due the credit union can be deducted from your paycheck automatically and paid by the district. This felicitous arrangement enables the credit union to make you an unsecured loan of up to $300 your first year in the district, and greater amounts after you're on tenure. Larger loans are available to new teachers with appropriate collateral. Later on, the credit union will finance your master's degree, your furniture, and summer camp for your kids. You'll never have a better friend.

Building Orientation

Meanwhile, in another part of the forest, orientation meetings are still going on. At your school, your principal will conduct the meetings and will introduce the counselors, the librarian, the school nurse, and probably the attendance secretary. You will already know about these people, because you will have come across them in your teachers' handbook. This introduction in the flesh will give you their names (take notes) and an idea of which points they wish to emphasize.

This is the time to ask questions. If you see discrepancies that puzzle you, ask about them. If you don't understand why a certain operation is done a certain way, ask; you may have to explain to new students. If you aren't sure which teacher functions are optional and which are mandatory, ask. If the handbook tells you this, that, or the other event will be held "in the theater" and on your diagram of the school you are unable to locate a theater, find out where it is. It's easier to ask than to wander about aimlessly for weeks hunting a place, especially if your school is a thirty-acre Xanadu with four gyms and two football fields.

Department Orientation

After you are dismissed from your school orientation meeting, you may be expected to go into a huddle with your department head. Expected to or not, you'd be well advised to hunt him up.

Whereas every school, regardless of size or location, has a principal who functions as undisputed top banana, the role of the department head will vary from school to school. The person in charge of your department may receive a substantial extra stipend in addition to his salary as a teacher, and devote most of his school day to administrative and supervisory duties. His stamp of approval may have been necessary before you were hired, in fact; and whether or not you are rehired every year until you make tenure may depend on his evaluation of your teaching. At the other extreme, he may have only the department head label and no duties beyond sorting and rerouting the mail.

Showing too little deference to the administrative department head can be a professional blunder, but showing too much deference to a mail clerk who may already be smarting under the indignity of his meaningless title, may be interpreted by him as sarcasm and could earn you a lifelong enemy. Proceed with care. It would be a shrewd idea to probe, tactfully, in order to discover where between these two extremes of authority you will find your man. ("If I want to ask about teaching something that might be controversial, should I talk to you or to the principal?")

If the department head is being paid to function as an administrator, he will be the one who carries the responsibility for the success or failure of the department. If this is the way the wind blows, he'll go to great lengths to help you; whereas, if he is merely a senior teacher with neither authority nor responsibility, he might lend you some bird prints for your bulletin board, smile warmly, and continue about his own business, leaving you to whitewash your share of the fence by yourself.

Perhaps you prefer the latter situation on the ground that it's twice as hard to please two bosses; but, of course, the matter is as broad as it's long. The more bosses, the more help.

If there is an administrator at the head of your department, you would be wise to observe a protocol of sorts. Take all problems and questions to your department head first. If he sends you to higher-ups, fine. Keep him informed about good things as well as bad. Don't let it be the head of another department who tells him about the student in your class who won a cup for the city-wide public speaking competition. Give him the pleasure of being able to spread the news himself.

Your department head will be the one who'll tell you the method used for apportioning classroom sets of textbooks. Be sure you understand which ones you should issue to students and which ones are to remain in the classroom for supplementary use. If your department head says you will use such-and-such a textbook, and that you may take your copies whenever you like, get them to your room as soon as possible. Borrow a dolly from the custodian or from the librarian. You will issue textbooks to your students the second or third day of classes, not the first. There is too much confusion the first day of school to attend to the job properly.

Which Boss?

Especially if you are teaching in a district with a thousand teachers or better, you are likely to run into a plethora of bosses, which will confuse you. It will seem to you that you are taking orders from your department head, your vice-principal, your principal, your supervisor, the assistant superintendent in charge of secondary schools, and the superintendent.

As a new teacher, you will get the impression you are also expected to "follow the suggestions of" (take orders, second class) the registrar, the head custodian, the librarian, the nurse, the counselors, the dean of boys, the dean of girls, and the audio-visual director. When you look around for somebody you can give orders to, or even make suggestions to, you won't find anybody but the students. And if you happen to teach a president of the student body, a captain of the football team, or an editor of the school paper, there may be some of your own students who will try to pull rank on you!

If you let it—and, most unfortunately, there are new teachers who do let it—this state of affairs can put you on the defensive to the point that you feel you must ask someone's permission before using the plumbing facilities in the teachers' lounge. There are entirely too many teachers, both old and new, who feel this way. They are intimidated by an educational bureaucracy that was erected for the sole purpose of supporting them in the classroom and, beyond that, has no other excuse for existing at all. Most of the people who make up the bureaucracy, in fact, would be the first to point this out.

There are people whose orders you should take, for excellent reasons. In matters pertaining to the school as a whole, you should take orders from the principal. He's captain of the team. If a team is going to accomplish anything by way of organized effort, someone must assume the responsibility for calling the plays.

You should take orders from your department head for the same reason you take orders from your principal. His area of authority is narrower; that is the only difference. What he chooses to do or not to do about the district supervisor in your teaching field should be up to him. Follow his lead.

These are the only people you should take orders from; and you have more to gain by submitting to their authority, no matter how much you may disagree with their decisions, than by flouting it.

There are, in addition, a number of people who are specialists in their fields, and you will consult them as the occasion demands. The librarian, the nurse, the registrar, the audio-visual people, and the counselors fall into this category. You are not compelled to follow the advice of these people about their respective specialties. You would merely be a little silly if you didn't, just as people who don't follow the advice of their physicians and lawyers are a little silly.

The most important specialist who falls into this last category is the person (or persons) on your school staff— an assistant principal or the dean of boys and the dean of girls—who handles the school's disciplinary problems. You will be learning a great deal in this area, and you will need strong support until you have learned it. You will require the help and advice of this person far more than he will need you. Your relationship to him should be that of pupil to teacher. Give him half a chance and he will make a pro out of you. Ignore him at your peril!

The Mail

To get back to more immediate concerns, have you located the mailboxes in the front office? If not, ask a secretary where they are and find your own box. This is where you will pick up the daily notices, reminders, and questionnaires that you are expected to read and act on promptly if action is indicated. Is your name at the top or the bottom of the cubicle? You'll want to read and act on *your* notices only, not somebody else's.

The Duplicating Machine

Examine the duplicating machine with a secretary. There will always be a spirit duplicator for teacher use. Later, when school is in session, you will have to run off your copies in a hurry, since another teacher will usually be waiting to use the machine when you finish. Try to get your duplicating needs for the first two weeks taken care of before the first day of school. That way, you can take more time in working the machine until you are sure you know how to operate it. The first few times, borrow an old spirit master from one of the secretaries and run it through first to see how the machine works. This procedure might save a master sheet that you have worked hours on.

Professional Organizations

Sometime before classes start, or soon thereafter, you will have to decide what to do about joining a professional organization. Unless there is some extenuating circumstance, don't pass up this opportunity. You will gain several advantages by joining.

The first advantage is getting to know other people in your district. You will get to know the people in your own school as a matter of course, but, as the months pass, you will want to widen your professional horizons. The best way to do this is to offer your services for committee work in your professional organization.

The second advantage is economical. By paying a few dollars to join, you save many dollars through special auto insurance rates, hospitalization plans, annuity plans, and, in some cases, discounts on goods and services in the community. By joining, you become a paying member of the group that negotiates with the school board for changes in the salary schedule, working conditions, and school district policies about sick leave and sabbaticals.

The third advantage is long-term. Are you hoping someday to become a supervisor, a dean of girls, a principal, or a superintendent? The best administrative training ground you will find will be in your professional organization. It is there that you will be able to discover whether you have the characteristics necessary to become an educational leader. If you do have these characteristics, it is also the place where you will have the best opportunity to develop them.

Which professional organization you choose to join is a matter of preference. If you have no preference, go with the crowd; join the one with the most members.

two

Get Set To Teach

The alarm clock rings on the morning of your first day of school. If you launch this fateful day by salting your breakfast coffee and sugaring your eggs, don't be unduly concerned. Such behavior is par for the course for the new teacher. Nerves. Just nerves. You will forget about teaching for today, remember. That will come later.

Beginning today, when the new fall schedule goes into operation, you will become involved in a series of experiences that will grow more bewildering as the school year progresses. Before September is over, you'll wonder what you got yourself into. Although your training was in teaching, and you thought this was what the district men had in mind when they employed you, you will be doing many other things in addition to teaching. Of every fifty-minute class period, in fact, you will put in about thirty minutes of actual teaching time. The rest of the time you will be attending to discipline, roll-checking, absence-slip-signing, pencil- and paper-lending, passing out books, and a ton of similar activities that have little or nothing to do with your chosen career. Bemused, you will wonder what happened to teaching.

Well, it went thataway. It's hard for us to comprehend just how old-fashioned our schools really are. Charles Dickens (1850) complained of the authoritarian teacher and the monotony of the classroom. Today, the high school student has several authoritarian teachers in an assortment of monotonous classrooms one hour wide by eighteen weeks long.

Carlton Washborne (1920) complained of, and for awhile was able to do something about, the school's failure to allow for individual differences. As a result, the nation saw the promising beginnings of Winnetka Plans and Dalton Plans during the prosperous years before the '29 crash. But the Depression nipped all that in the bud, and we were soon back where we started.

You can't pick up a professional book or magazine nowadays that doesn't contain at least one article damning the American secondary school. There are as many diagnoses of the trouble as there are educational leaders, and the hideous truth is that all of them are probably correct. You ran into discussions of most of these problems in your teacher training courses, but a brief rundown may help you connect what you studied with what you will be experiencing in your classes:

1. We teach courses, not students. You will reach 60 per cent of the students in your classes. The work will be too easy or too hard for the other 40 per cent, who will sit there and fester. This state of affairs won't exist because you are lazy, but because that's the way the system is set up to operate. If you decide you're going to teach students instead of courses, you'll be in for trouble—not people trouble, organization trouble. (For individualizing instruction in your own class, see page 34.)

2. Today's teen-ager requires a different kind of education than his grandfather had, because he has been conditioned by TV, films, and urban sprawl. As a flaming youth in the '20's, his grandfather didn't like school either, and, if the opportunity arose, he also instigated free-for-alls in the

lunchroom. What gives today's teen-ager his aura of menace is that there are more of him in the population at large. Multiply that lunchroom rumble by a hundred, and you don't have boyish pranks any more; you have minor insurrection.

3. The high school has never developed a working rationale of its own. Philosophically, it borrows from the elementary school and mollycoddles students too old to be mollycoddled, or it borrows from the university and flunks out students too young to be flunked out. You will find that the burden of responsibility is on you to teach in spite of everything, rather than on the students to learn in spite of everything. At grading time, you'll be in hot water from parents, students, and administrators if you don't show a curve, or something close to it. This situation will be frustrating to you. It will also frustrate your students, who express their disapproval by sassing teachers and planting bombs in lockers.

4. Classes are too big. In the years to come, Great Society or no Great Society, teachers will be increasingly reluctant to put down roots in systems where their classes average thirty-five students or more.

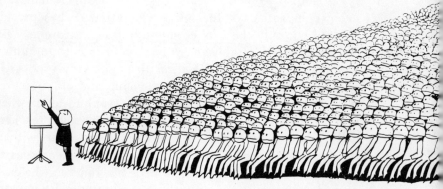

5. The curriculum is unrealistic. Your textbooks will be out-of-date. Make do with magazines and newspapers to fill in the gaps. When it comes to curriculum change, the school's

reaction time is something like five years. Five years isn't exactly charging ahead at a full gallop; but when you consider that before the curriculum can be changed, books must be printed, states and counties must okay their adoption, and old textbooks must be used up before new ones can be purchased, you must admit it's a respectable trot. If society wants its young to be educated realistically, it will have to co-operate by slowing down a bit. What can be done, and needs to be done, in the schools, is to teach students to teach themselves and convince them it's worth the trouble.

NB

6. The class-plus-teacher educational unit has outlived its usefulness, and new modes of organizing for instruction must be developed. A teacher and his students form a social unit, yeasty and malleable. When these balls of social dough are stacked into the larger structure of the school, they no longer function as balls of dough, but as bricks, and they lose their effectiveness. You will have little opportunity to get to know your students and rejoice with them in their triumphs or commiserate with them in their sorrows. Instead, you will see hordes of faceless little people tramping in and out of your classroom, far more efficiently conditioned to the bell than Pavlov's dogs ever were. Self-service education sounds as outlandish to modern ears as self-service merchandising sounded in 1910; yet the self-service principle has revolutionized not only the U.S. economy but our culture as well. The educational Establishment has too little faith in human curiosity and far, far too little faith in the very product it sells, education. If all Americans, young and old, are ever turned loose to learn everything they want to learn when they want to learn it, our puny cadre of two million teachers will be swamped with the demand. The big schools are with us for good. In the end, however, if the economy continues to prosper and educators exercise a little imagination, the class as we know it will one day yield to something more human. The machines will help us do it, too. Wait and see. In the meantime, it will be your obligation to cope with the American high school, not as you hope it will be twenty-five years hence, but as it is now.

The First Day

For the first few days of your first year (or any year, for that matter), the standing rule for teachers is as inflexible as it is terse: Stay put and do as you're told. Believe me, it's simpler that way. If you attended all your meetings and listened, and if you did your homework, you should be able to remember fairly well all the things you were told to do.

The first day or two of school, expect the unexpected. Forty-five students may show up one period and six the next, and twenty may appear for a class during what you thought was to be your planning period. Expect wacky things to happen if your school is moving into computerized scheduling and attendance; things will go far more smoothly once the change has been made, but the transition period is murder. No matter how many students show up, or no matter when they show up, have them all come in and sit down; get it straightened out later in the office.

When students come to your room the first day of school, you should say something to them. The first thing you should say is, "My name is Mr. Hansen, and this is world history class," or whatever. There will be one or two students who will get up and walk out because they thought they were in Miss Haynes's algebra class. Direct them to the right room if you can.

Next, call the roll. You will have received, in some form, the names of students you should expect in each class. When you receive these names, it will be a temptation to alphabetize them and write them down immediately in your pretty new gradebook. Don't. Dozens of student changes will be made before classes at last begin to stabilize after you're well into the second week of school. Until then, improvise temporary class sheets with a ruler and graph paper. When you have conducted a class for a week without adding or subtracting students, you can then transpose the list of names to your gradebook with some assurance that the alphabetical arrangement will remain valid for a while. Keep your gradebook in pencil; you'll soon find out why.

The same advice applies to seating charts. Make temporary ones to start. Wait until later to fill in the seating chart
forms the school will give you, and then keep them in pencil.
Many teachers like to seat students in alphabetical order,
because it's easier to learn names that way. Be sure you keep
your seating charts up to date. Someday you will stay home
with the flu and your substitute will need them badly.

As you call the names of your students, make an effort
to get pronunciations and nicknames straight. If in doubt,
ask: "Do you want me to call you Richard or Dick?" Make
notes on your temporary class sheet. Begin as soon as
possible to link names and faces. The rambunctious boy in
the blue shirt who won't sit down when you tell him the first
day, will, you'll find, settle down immediately the second
day when you say, "Bill, sit down."

After you have called the names you were given, ask if
there were any names you did not call. There may be one or
two souls who are waiting to register until they have sampled
a class here and a class there, honeybee fashion, before they
go to the counselor to have their schedules made up. You
may have been given instructions about disposition of such
students. If you haven't, send them to the office to register.

It may happen that you don't receive class rosters from
the office before the first day of school and have no roll to
check, or at best an incomplete one. If this is the case, take
your first day's attendance by passing a sheet of lined paper
around the class for student signatures. In fact, if there is
important information you need from each student for your
records (his homeroom teacher, for example), you may want
to check attendance by this method even though you have
a roster to work from. While the attendance sheet is being
passed around the room, go ahead with your introductory
remarks. Fifteen minutes later, when the sheet has completed its circuit of the room, glance over it for signatures
you can't read. Be sure you can decipher the spellings of
difficult names correctly. Don't be surprised if you discover
Julius Caesar or Lyndon B. Johnson on the list. To learn
Caesar's real identity, check the names immediately pre-

ceding and following his on the list. The name just ahead of Caesar's is Paulena Headly. "Paulena? Will you raise your hand?" The name that follows Caesar's is Bill Lamson. "Bill Lamson? Where are you?" The clown seated between them is your target. "What's your name, buster?"

In teaching at the high school level, your most important assets are a thick skin and a sense of humor. Both will get an especially good workout these opening days of school.

Although a good teacher keeps his lectures to a minimum, the first day of school is an exception. Your students will feel more at ease if they know something about you, and you should talk about yourself. Your name should be written on the chalkboard. Say it slowly if it's hard to pronounce. Tell the students if you are married and have children. Tell them where you got your degree and when. If you have military experience or if you won awards or honors, tell them about it. Talk about your hobbies. If a student asks about your teaching experience, tell him about the school where you did your apprentice teaching and change the subject. Why advertise your innocence?

Show them what you can do. A music teacher might play a little jazz on the piano; a physical education teacher can demonstrate a difficult exercise; an English teacher might read a poem. This is a vitally important strategy for helping to control potential disciplinary problems. Students respect a pro.

If time allows, the first day, tell your students a little bit about what you expect to cover in the course. They will also want to know if you expect reports or themes, and how many. How much time will they be allowed for make-up work after

an absence? How often will you give tests? How much will
tests and reports count for grades? There will be groans of
anguish and vigorous testimonials to the effect that none of
the other teachers makes such stiff demands. Pay no attention. You will have gone over these points previously with
your department head to find out if they are consistent with
what the school usually expects of its students. Believe what
your department head tells you, not what the students tell
you.

By the end of the day, you'll be hoarse from talking nonstop since the first bell rang, but you may also be eager to
get started with your teaching now that you have had a look
at your students.

What Have We Here

The first week, at least, you will be "finding" your class.
How much can they do *now*? You will give a series of prelimi-
nary exercises to find the upper and lower ability limits of
your groups. Even if you have a one-preparation teaching
assignment, you will find no two groups to be exactly alike.
You won't need to prepare a new lesson plan for each class,
but count on adapting the plan you're using. Some classes
may be able to tackle difficult work more quickly than others.

You are sure to have at least one class with an unusually
wide range of ability. If you give a quiz of, say, ten questions,
and one or two students answer all the questions correctly,
but one or two students answer all the questions *in*correctly,
you have a difficult class to teach. Talk to the scheduling
people about the problem, especially if your school is ability-
grouped. Show them your students' papers. See if they will
reschedule a few of your more able students into a higher
section, or a few of your low-scoring students into basic
classes. Your aim is to narrow your range of student ability
in that class. If you aren't successful in making this exchange,
you might be forced to work separately with the top or
bottom 10 per cent of your students for whom your lesson
plan is simply not appropriate (see "Individualizing Instruc-

tion," page 34). Seasoned teachers sometimes handle this situation by grouping their students, but intra-class grouping is a difficult teaching technique for the beginning secondary school teacher to undertake. Both discipline and curriculum problems will trip him up. The same goes for individualizing all the work in your class. Don't try to hoe more than one row of corn at a time at the start.

Instruction: A Working Technique

As your school concludes the initial scheduling phase and everyone more or less settles down to teaching and learning, it will be time to put the finishing touches on lesson plans for your first two or three weeks. When you sit down with your course of study and your borrowed final examination to plot out what you will do with your classes, you will undoubtedly plan presentations and projects that fall into the "show biz" category. Typically, the new teacher thinks in terms of unusual ways to tell or show things to the students. He gives cursory attention to, or forgets altogether,

turn to Chapter four

Page 33

how *they* are going to *tell him* what they are learning, or how he is going to go about correcting the errors they will most surely make. To his chagrin, he will give a test at the end of his first fancy unit and discover his students haven't learned anything at all!

What went wrong? Well, he put on a good vaudeville act. The students may have sat spellbound or toppled from their seats with laughter, but they weren't taught. It's not the same thing.

A useful cracker-barrel rule for teaching is: I tell you, you tell me, and I tell you if you're wrong. What the rule lacks in sophistication, it makes up for in effectiveness—it works. Project the film for your class on the ceiling, if you insist; but once you've made the point you wanted to get across, have the students paraphrase or repeat that point to you in some way, and tell them if they got it right or not.

There are hundreds of variations on the "I tell you, you tell me, and I tell you if you're wrong" plan. You will readily see this if you use your prep period occasionally to observe and analyze the work of experienced teachers. If you can't spare your prep period, watch master teachers on educational television.

"I tell you" could be assigned textbook reading, a multimedia presentation, or a laboratory demonstration. "You tell me" could be a quiz, a panel discussion, or a research paper. "I tell you if you're wrong" could be a corrected test paper plus a discussion of the test questions, or your summary and evaluation of a class project.

The most successful "I tell you if you're wrong" is when the teacher is able to structure the situation so the student himself finds out what's wrong, but it isn't always possible to do this, unfortunately.

One trip through the cycle is seldom sufficient to bring about the necessary learning. You will notice that the amount of reteaching required for mastery will depend on the existing knowledge of the students. If the concept being taught (adverbs, for example) is simply an extension or modification of concepts already mastered (adjectives), the new idea can be grasped more quickly.

As you gain skill in using this formula with your classes, you will find you can arrange your teaching in either inductive or deductive sequences. Your students are more apt to "discover" what you want them to if you have exercised the proper care in teaching the elements leading up to it. Even lessons devoted to problem-solving will be more successful if you teach the problem and the pertinent facts contributing to it before you send your students to search for possible solutions.

You must also develop the sensitivity to be able to tell when the student is teaching himself, and to judge if he is doing an efficient job of it. If and when he is, you're the one who gets the A!

There are many more skills that we teach ourselves than are taught us by other people. You will teach yourself how to improve your teaching. You will hear of a good idea you might use in your classroom (Step 1); you will try it with your students (Step 2); and you will decide if you have or have not done it properly and modify your behavior accordingly (Step 3). It is precisely this skill, the ability to teach oneself, that the successful teacher works toward and ultimately imparts to his students. At the higher level of instruction, in fact, the successful teacher, in or out of the classroom, is one who inspires his students to teach themselves.

Poor timing is a booby trap to avoid. Ideally, presentation, recitation, and knowledge of results—all three of your teaching steps—should take place within one class period. It is better to risk a little inefficient checking and have students check their own papers, or exchange and check each other's work, than to wait until the next day to let the students know how well they learned the material. However, don't make a steady practice of student checking. You will decide how much new material to present, depending on what the students are or are not learning. Accurate information is something you simply *must* have in order to gauge this properly. Go over test questions with your students as soon as possible after you have administered the test, even though you have not yet graded all the test papers.

In using the "I tell you, etc." formula with group instruction, you must decide at what point most of the students have achieved mastery before you proceed to new material. In view of your allotted life span, it isn't prudent to keep reteaching the same material until everybody in the class gets it. If between 50 and 75 per cent achieve mastery, it's time to go on to new material for a few days. Return to the old material next week for a thorough review (reteaching) and pick up another 10 per cent of your students. If there are curriculum points that are crucially important, come back again next month. Don't hope to bring 100 per cent of your students to mastery. You'll never do it.

Review, or reteaching the most important points, serves two other, more important purposes. First, it insures that learned material won't be forgotten. Second, it builds the student's over-all perspective of what he's doing. As the bits of learned material fall into place, the student begins to develop a total concept, which in itself tends to encourage him toward greater efforts.

Individualizing Instruction

Many experienced teachers have tried to individualize instruction in their classrooms at one time or another. The attempts are often unsuccessful. They are so very unsuccessful, in fact, that nostrils flare in distaste at the thought of trying it again.

Individually-paced instruction is philosophically incompatible with group-paced instruction. Trying to juggle both of these techniques in the same classroom with the same students at the same time is a little like trying to graft the front end of a mackerel to the tail end of a chicken. Not only are the advantages of individual work lost ("swamped out," as the systems engineers call it), but an entirely new set of disadvantages arises.

If you isolate a few students and give them work that is entirely different from the rest of the class, the few students you have singled out soon begin to feel like outsiders and lose their enthusiasm. If you compel a few students to do assignments over and above their classroom tasks for no extra credit, they feel overworked and underpaid, and they balk. If you allow a few students to do extra assignments and give them extra credit toward their grades, the rest of the class will demand and, in justice, should be given—the same privilege. All the time this is going on, you are preparing a lesson plan for each individually-paced student *in addition to* the lesson plan you are preparing for your class. Keeping these arrangements going any length of time requires as much in the way of statesmanship as in teaching prowess.

Later on in your teaching career, you will be more familiar with school procedures. You will have taught with your curriculum materials for a year or so and will know their strengths and weaknesses. Then, if you are fortunate enough to have classes of no more than twenty-five students, you may want to individualize *all* of your instruction—but not just some of it, and not for a week or two, but for the entire school year. This is a different matter. Study plans to accommodate the range of ability in your classes can be developed (interesting ones, or the whole thing falls apart) and run off on the duplicating machine. Teacher-student conferences can be scheduled on a weekly basis.

There are advantages for the student in individualized instruction. His work is more interesting, because he can *do* it. Since classroom logistics are individualized as well as the instruction, the student's study effort need not be delayed while other students locate their books and find the place; thus, the student spends more net time at his learning tasks. He develops self-reliance because the teacher is no longer holding his lollipop for him and telling him when to lick. He learns how to manage and improve his own study habits. Because he is happier in his work, disciplinary problems decrease, leaving more time for study and learning. Most important of all, he learns more.

There are advantages for you, too. You stop behaving like a mechanical toy and start behaving like a human being. There is more opportunity to use your imagination and intelligence, and less need to bark like a drill sergeant. As to

physical effort, it isn't any harder than teaching classes; many times, it's easier. You stop thinking in terms of forest management and start thinking in terms of tree management —you get to know kids, not classes.

In the meantime, you're going to have some students in your classes who will finish their work before the others and get nearly all of the answers right, and other students who will never finish anything and will get the problems all wrong. They will bother you. What can you do?

Frankly, if you are carrying a total load of 150 students or more, you'd better not do anything. You'll only short-circuit yourself and disappoint your students if you try. As a beginning teacher, you'll accomplish more if you concentrate your time and energy on competent, thorough, day-to-day class instruction and resist the temptation to slice yourself into ineffectual slivers. You must choose the lesser of two evils here; you are trading off individual work with a few students to insure competent instruction for the larger number.

Should you be fortunate enough to have a load of a hundred students or less, however, and find you have extra time you can devote to unusually slow or unusually bright students in your classroom, you may suggest extra books and projects for them. The operation will proceed more smoothly if you assign this as a substitute homework assignment or perhaps, as work to be done in your class after the student finishes his regular class assignments. If you are forced to, offer extra credit to keep the student working.

Attempts to individualize instruction break down if the teacher doesn't follow up his assignments as he should. He will attend to Step 1 of the "I tell you" formula with a flourish, but finds himself running short of time to attend to Steps 2 and 3 properly. Have the student set his own deadlines and insist that he meet them. Have him tell you what he read or show you what he did (Step 2). Correct his work and explain matters he may not understand (Step 3). Remember, in the case of the slow student there will be no voluntary admission from him that there are things he doesn't understand. You will have to probe to find these weak spots.

The Textbook and Its Uses

"Teaching the book" isn't very sophisticated pedagogy, and the result can be a dreary series of lessons untouched by the human mind. But it needn't be this way, and the process of learning to teach is far simpler if the first-year teacher has a textbook and is held accountable for teaching little beyond what's within its covers. Such a strategy is less taxing on a beginner's meager store of experience than combining fifty or more pamphlets, books, filmstrips, etc., to present a course of study "creatively." In the hands of the novice, what starts out as "creative teaching" often ends up as nine months of gong banging.

The textbook is there. Everybody has a copy (no logistics problems). The content is organized (no sequencing problems). There is a feeling of starting here and ending there, of getting down to business, which is preferable to the sense of aimless wandering that sometimes results when the teacher builds his course of study from many different sources.

There are worse sins than "teaching the book" and supplementing it with exercises, work at the chalkboard, and an occasional phonograph record or film. No one needs to apologize for a modest teaching effort performed with diligence and care. As you gain experience, you can attempt more ambitious techniques with less likelihood of failure.

Your textbook can serve you as a valuable tool and faithful friend if you use it with respect. Undermining the confidence of young students in the authority of the textbook can boomerang. "The ignoramus who wrote this book says it's all right to end a sentence with a preposition because Winston Churchill did. The textbook is wrong. I'm afraid the rules of correct usage are stricter than that. At least in *this* classroom, they will be." Thus admonished, a teacher's students won't end sentences with prepositions; neither will they use verbs or form plurals the way the textbook writer

suggests, even though the teacher *does* agree with the writer
on the latter points. As far as the students are concerned,
the textbook writer can drop dead. What does *he* know?

Of course, particularly in the area of science, there will be
times when the textbook *is* wrong. It may be out of date.
When this happens, assign the parts of the text that are still
valid, and bring in other sources for the rest. The shrewd
teacher won't make a federal case of it.

Multiple Exposure

Your first year in the classroom, you will observe a common
phenomenon that plays an important part in the way students grasp new information. A student will seldom absorb
a fact from one media alone—the textbook, for example,
even a programmed one—and remember it very long. The
mind seems to function much as the eyes or the ears do. If
we see something with only one eye, we don't "know" that
visual image as thoroughly as we do when we see it with both
eyes. Seeing it with both eyes gives an additional dimension
to our understanding. For example, students will remember
better how our nation's judicial process works if they read
it in the textbook and later see a film illustrating the various
types of cases that are handled in different courts of law.

Experienced teachers arrange for multiple exposure (com-
munications people call it redundance) of learning materials

when they supplement textbook study with pertinent magazine and newspaper articles, with models, and with realia. The shrewder ones also present homework assignments with multiple exposure in mind; they tell the students what is expected *and* they write the assignment in a designated place on the chalkboard.

Discussion

The most commonly employed activity to ensure multiple exposure is "discussing" material that has previously been read by the class. There are two distinctly different kinds of discussion: oral recitation and informal debate. Both are valuable, but for different reasons.

In one case out of ten, the teacher who says, "We're going to discuss the assignment," intends to have the students debate the pros and cons of the lesson among themselves. More often, what he means is that he will catechize the students about what they have or have not read ("What did the parsley garden have to do with the story?" "What committees would review this bill before it came to the floor of the House?").

A hundred years ago, this catechizing activity was not only the most popular teaching technique, it was virtually the *only* teaching technique in use. Good horses, unfortunately, are the ones in most danger of being ridden to death. By the time of the Progressives, oral recitation had fallen into disrepute. Fortunately for all of us, the practice refused to die.

Today teachers ask their students more sophisticated questions. For example, we use the technique to establish mental set ("Today we're going to read a story entitled *The Most Dangerous Game*. What will it be about, do you suppose?" "Bob, before we go on to special safety devices, will you review the safety rules we studied yesterday?"), to promote transfer of learning ("How would you install this brake lining in your own car, Ed?" "Can someone give us an example of an everyday problem that could be solved by doing what this hero did?"), and to encourage the formulation of conclusions and inferences ("What's likely to happen to AB if you double CD but cut EF in half?" "Does the author like Swedes or not? What leads you to think so?"). But the teacher is still on the asking end, and students are still on the answering end. Today, we call it "class discussion."

Oral recitation, alias class discussion, is valuable, because it performs two instructional functions at once. From the point of view of the teaching formula already mentioned, the textbook gives the student his information (Step 1), he repeats what he has read to the teacher (Step 2), and he is corrected if he is mistaken, or given additional information if it appears to be needed (Step 3). Equally important, while this question-and-answer dialogue is going on between the teacher and individual students, the other class members are hearing a paraphrased version of the important points of the lesson, which in itself gives them a surer grasp of the material.

This kind of "discussion" is still as badly overworked as ever, probably because it's so easy. The only equipment required for student use is one textbook and one mouth each, neither of which must be checked out from the library or the audio-visual department. But there are other, equally effective ways to achieve the same results, and they should also be used.

Informal debate—a hot controversy between evenly-matched student opponents, both of whom have done their homework and know what they're talking about—is as provocative to witness as a major league football game. When

the teacher specifies that members of the audience may participate in the fracas, provided they have also looked up their sources and are sure of their statistics, you have all three steps of the teaching formula working for you at the same time. Since the prize goes to the students who have learned the most and presented what they learned most effectively, you have a superb learning situation.

How marvelous it would be if all of us were skillful enough to engineer this kind of verbal jousting! A great deal of skill, of course, is required to bring it off. Students don't do it automatically; they must be trained to do it. Training involves giving up childish values and adopting mature ones; it means forsaking "what I feel to be true" and substituting "what I know to be true." In essence, it means growing up. Let's face it, people who are good at bringing about this kind of behavior in their fellow human beings are rare. Yet, it's an ideal we all can and should strive to achieve.*

The Dynamics of Pacing

Another phenomenon the teacher must take into account if he is to achieve his teaching objectives quickly and consistently has to do with pacing. If you keep your students hard at work on difficult concepts for several days running, you'll find interest and effort beginning to lag. The same is true if you spend too much time on tasks that are below your students' normal level of achievement. But if you vary the diet of moderately difficult assignments by arranging your lesson plans so that you occasionally introduce both easier and more difficult work, you build into your teaching viable qualities that might not otherwise be there.

Even within one scheduled period, give some thought to the amount of tension engendered by the tasks you assign. Twenty minutes of intense student concentration should be relieved by twenty minutes of work requiring less effort. From time to time, spend fifteen minutes on a drill of material

*See William M. Sattler and N. Edd Miller, *Discussion and Conference*, Englewood Cliffs, N.J.: Prentice-Hall, Inc., 1954, especially Chapters 9, 10, and 11.

already learned, or show a film dealing with concepts studied briefly in your class but designed for use at the college level (warn your students ahead of time that they may not understand a lot of it). By occasionally introducing learning tasks both above and below normal grade-level, you give your students a "sense of place" in the subject matter. They have a clearer idea of where they've been and where they're going.

Questions

Your students will look to you as a source of information— "When did the Romans invade Gaul?" "Who the heck was Aristophanes?" "What do those dots mean?" Try to recognize student questions for what they are, and dispose of them accordingly.

The farther down the socio-intellectual scale your student, the more important it is for you to encourage him in asking you questions. The culturally-deprived student rarely forms the habit at home of seeking information from authority figures. His questions indicate quickening curiosity and trust, both of which are firm steps in the right direction. Give him an answer to the question he asks, but resist the temptation to deliver an unsolicited lecture or overwhelm him with information about dictionaries and encyclopedias; he isn't ready to handle it yet.

Another kind of questioner will be the student who is ready to be led to find new sources of information, such as biographical encyclopedias, a thesaurus, shop manuals, and so on. Either show him yourself ("Let's go look . . .") or tell him exactly where to look.

There is another kind of questioner. He is the knowledgeable student who is well aware of where to find the information; he is using you to save wear and tear on his feet. If you have time, accommodate him as a favor to a friend; otherwise, tell him to go look it up himself.

Never, *never* refuse information to a student who sincerely needs it and sincerely doesn't know where else to get it. This is the crime of crimes for the teacher to commit.

Vocabulary

Vocabulary building is every teacher's business. The richer and more varied the student's fund of words, the more knowledge of all kinds he is potentially capable of mastering. Any student, regardless of his intellect, will be more likely to add a word to his permanent vocabulary if he hears it pronounced and used in a sentence. You shouldn't, therefore, be content to present printed lists of technical terms and their definitions to your students. Use the word in your lecture—not once, but several times. Require the students to use the word, both orally and in writing. All else failing, have them sing it out in unison. Not until a student uses the word himself is it truly his own property.

Now Hear This!

Nothing spooks kids as much as the compulsive order-giver: "All right, now, students, let's take out our books. Okay? No, Harry, not that book, your math book. Sue, where's your book? Get it out on top of your desk; we're going to do an exercise now. That's fine. Everybody have their books? Okay. Now turn to page 115. Page 115. You have page 115, Gerald? Let's see. All right. Now that's not the right page, Marie. Page one-one-five—115. You have page 115, Francine? Got it? Okay. Everybody's turned to page 115. Now, see the row of equations in the middle of the page? Not the bottom of the page, the middle. Row B, middle of page 115, etc."

This kind of flapping at the mouth produces poor behavior patterns. To retain his sanity, the student has no choice but to tune you out, to ignore you. Teachers complain that students don't listen. The reason students don't listen is that, by such thoughtless chattering, we teachers have *taught* them not to listen.

After two or three days of being treated like four-year-olds, your students will begin to fight back. They will plague you by *behaving* like four-year-olds, upon which you will find

yourself giving still more orders. And the more orders you give, the fewer will be obeyed.

Do you really want your students to listen to you? Then button your lip. Write assignments. on the chalkboard: "Today's assignment, textbook, p. 115, Row B. Work all four problems." Then circulate among your students so you will be available if they have questions to ask.

"*I*" Defects

Another guaranteed method of making every single one of your students ignore every single thing you say is to begin every single sentence with "I"—"I want you to write a paragraph," "I want to tell you about the properties of copper," "I want to warn you about this electric saw."

A tip that any salesman will give you, free, is that the pronoun "you" penetrates more skulls than "I"—"You have all the information you need to write your paragraph," "You will need to know about the properties of copper," "If you aren't careful, this electric saw will slice you up like a side of bacon."

Stay in Your Own Yard

Resist the temptation to add whimsical touches to your course of study until you are more experienced and know your fellow teachers well enough to work out special teaching arrangements with them. English teachers shouldn't unilaterally decide to teach folk dancing, for example, because the gym teachers already teach it and they won't appreciate your horning in, unannounced, on their curriculum.

The Broken Promise and the Sickly Smile

"I have the very book you need at home; I'll bring it for you tomorrow." "The new beakers have been ordered and they'll be here next week." "There aren't any more copies of the bibliography, but I'll run off more this afternoon."

"Oh, that *book* I told you about! Ha-ha-ha. Yes, it's still at home. I'll bring it tomorrow, I promise." "Well, I can't *imagine* what could have happened to those beakers." "Silly old me! It's been three weeks and I just *can't* remember to run off those copies of the bibliography!"

If your students can't believe what you say about the book or the beakers or the bibliography, they won't believe what you say about syntax or binomials, either. If you don't intend to deliver, or if there's a possibility others will make a liar out of you, don't promise.

Controversial Subjects

Somewhere along the line, you will have to make up book lists and topics for themes and reports for the students. This brings us into a sensitive area. The question of whether such subjects as rape, racial intermarriage, legalized prostitution, and abortion are appropriate for classroom consideration is beyond the scope of this book. It is well within the scope of this book to warn you that these subjects, and others like them, can produce unpleasant reverberations in the community. The experienced teacher who has already won the respect of both parents and students will be more likely to pick his way over this delicate terrain without detonating land mines. The inexperienced teacher should ask for advice and proceed cautiously.

Base your assignments on a choice of topics rather than on one topic—"The Negro and His Ghetto," "The Puerto Rican's Drive for Identity," "The Plight of the Navajo Indian," "Growing Up White in Twentieth-century America." Even with a choice, leave the door open to add others to the list pending teacher approval. (The English teacher can assign interesting theme topics ad infinitum without offending anyone's political, religious or social tastes—"Is He Too Old for Her?" "How Much Protection Do My Parents Owe Me?" "The Day I Grew Up.")

The same rule applies to books. Assign readings from a list of several titles. You can't go wrong by using books on the list the American Library Association publishes annually, although even then there will be some crackpot parent who will "raise Cain" because you made his daughter read a sinful book like *Lost Horizon* (the hero enters a bar and orders a drink on page 2). He'll ask you, "Why can't you have students read the classics, like Shakespeare?" Stay out of it. Let the principal handle it.

I Read It Already!

Don't be intimidated by students who will, as sure as you're born, insist that "I already read that book" or "We did that project last year." When a student says this, his motive will be to raise his status in the eyes of classmates who may be within earshot, not to lend a constructive hand in your curriculum decisions. If you talk to the student privately, he will more readily admit it was Book One of the series he studied last year, not the Book Two you have for him this year. He may have studied one chapter only of Book Two in summer school. He may also have read a watered-down version of a classic or a *Reader's Digest* condensation of some book on your list. Don't abandon your plans or modify your lists without researching the problem a bit. If it turns out that one of your hundred-odd students has already read some of the books on your list, simply tell him to choose a title he hasn't read.

Lesson Plans

You will already have prepared and worked from lesson plans in your student teaching course, and will have begun to develop a feel for the kind of plan that is most helpful for your own subject and classroom procedure.

Vogues in education, like vogues in women's fashions, come and go. Earlier in the century, the Progressive educators stated teaching objectives in behavioral terms, a practice that is once again "in." What's the difference? Well, instead of saying you're going to teach students to recognize and use subordinate clauses correctly, which, you must admit, leaves something to be desired in the way of precision, you say you want your students to score 70 per cent or better on a twenty-item quiz in which the student will identify and construct subordinate clauses. This twenty-item quiz, incidentally, will represent Step 2 of your final teaching cycle of the day's lesson.

In addition to your teaching objectives, your lesson plan should include a brief statement of what you intend to do and what you intend to have the students do, and a list of the things the students are going to work with, look at, listen to, read, carve, or dismantle.

A word of caution: Even if you are lucky enough to have a larynx made of vinyl and can talk nonstop for three hours without tiring, don't, for heaven's sake, schedule any forty-

five minute lectures in your lesson plans. Few people can
bat the breeze so engagingly that teen-agers will listen to
them for that long. You'll do a better job of teaching, and
your students will do a better job of learning, if you break
up your instruction periods with two or three different
activities, only one of which could be your lecture. You'll do
a better job still, if *none* of the activities is a lecture.

Your lesson plans may be checked occasionally by your
department head. Your school will provide a lesson plan
book as a convenience to you. The book, together with the
plans you write in it, is considered your property. Perhaps
you will prefer to keep your lesson plans on 9" x 5" cards or
in a loose-leaf binder of your own. This will be acceptable
in the majority of cases, as long as you leave clear instructions
for your substitute should you become ill.

Some schools require teachers to file lesson plans a week
ahead of time, in which case you will simply make carbon
copies of the plans you write out for your own use. The plan-
filing requirement is in effect because of the irritating habit
teachers (older ones, usually) have of carrying lesson plans
around between their ears instead of in a book where a
substitute could find them.

There's small chance that you, as a new teacher, will be
guilty of such thoughtlessness. Your first attempt to teach
"off the top of your head" will produce such unpleasant
results that you'll quickly retreat to carefully thought-out,
written plans. Let's hope your retreat will be a permanent
one. Improvised lesson plans are like home movies; only

members of the immediate family should be subjected to them.

There is something else you can do to make things easier for a substitute teacher. Clip a sheet of "Information for Substitutes" inside the cover of your lesson plan book or gradebook. On it, list general information: your schedule, customary classroom procedures, title of the textbook and most commonly used supplementary books, location of teachers' manuals and answer keys, seating charts, and location of the radiator knob (no, I'm not kidding). The more information you leave your substitute, the more mileage you will get out of him.

Memorizing

Sooner or later, the time will come when you must require your students to memorize something. It may be a school song, a speech for the P.T.A. program, or how to say "supercalifragilisticexpialidocious." Don't command them to memorize it and abandon them; show them how:

1. Read or sing the entire piece to show them how it goes.
2. Break the total material to be memorized into sections. No section should require longer than five seconds to say (or yell, or sing, or chant.)
3. Memorize Section A.
4. After Section A has been mastered, memorize B.
5. Review A and B together several times.
6. Learn Section C.
7. Learn Section D.
8. Review CD.
9. Review ABCD.
10. Add E, then F. Review EF.
11. Add G, H. Review GH. Review EFGH.
12. Review ABCDEFGH, etc.

Maybe you've been assigned to sponsor the pompon girls and you must teach them a dance to go with a song or yell. First of all, show them the entire routine. Then have the girls sit down, well spaced out, and teach them everything from the waist up—words, tune, and arm-shoulder-head movements. Teach it thoroughly. Then start all over, a section at a time, and add the legs.

Lists of technical terms and foreign language vocabulary should be handled differently. Encourage your students to work in pairs, taking turns at reciting to each other. Words must be given randomly, not in straight sequence. Student teams should begin with two or three words, adding new ones and dropping old ones as mastery is achieved. Cardboard flash cards or transparent slides projected briefly on a screen (tachistoscope-style) are valuable teaching aids for work of this kind. Slides are preferable to filmstrips because the order can be changed and new words can be added and old ones dropped as they are mastered. You, yourself, should make certain that students are able to use the terms correctly in context.

Homework

Research findings on whether or not homework does any good are inconclusive. One suspects they reflect the preconceived notions of the researchers, and, since the researchers don't agree, the results don't.

Whether or not you assign homework, and how much, will depend on several factors. (These factors are as relevant as all get-out to the teacher in the classroom, but, for some curious reason, never seem to be relevant to the researchers who write up the studies.) You may, of course, be teaching subjects such as art or shop, where homework isn't customary because students don't have the necessary equipment at home to do it; or, because of extremely heavy pupil load, homework may require so much supervisory time that you can't keep the homework assignments going and take care of your regular classroom instructional duties as well. You may be teaching slow, average, or college prep classes, in which case you will assign none, some, or a lot, respectively, depending on the intellectual ability of the students and the desires of their parents.

It isn't keeping ahead on grading homework exercises and drills that will put gray in your hair, for this can be done in class or by random checking procedures. What's difficult is keeping pressure on the laggards who don't turn their homework in. There isn't any easy way around this problem. If you're going to assign homework at all, you must arrange a system of rewards for those who get it in and penalties for those who don't; otherwise, no one will do it. But penalties and rewards won't automatically take care of the problem; neither will generous doses of scolding or pep talks about the value of education. Giving F's for failure to produce homework assignments furthers the objectives of a few students who hope to flunk out of school to even the score with Mom, Pop, the school, or society in general.

As common as the individual student who wants to flunk out for private reasons, is the situation where entire classes will embark on informal slowdown strikes and turn in only enough work of any kind, homework included, to get by with a D. The teacher can hound two or three students in a class, perhaps, or ten or twelve students from five classes, but personally hounding more than a hundred students just isn't practical.

So, what can the teacher do? If he gives the students time in class to do their homework, it isn't really homework any more, is it? Keeping the students after school runs into team practice, club meetings, or the bus schedule. No, there isn't any easy way out of it.

If assigned, homework should have a purpose. It should prepare the student for a class activity the following day or provide practice after the skill has first been learned at school. Used in this way, homework makes sense, and makes classroom work more meaningful. Under such circumstances, both the teacher and the students understand the value of homework and respect it—and you'll have a much better chance of getting the assignments back from all your students.

Avoid assigning homework regularly, like vitamin pills, "because it's good for you." You wouldn't take home a stack of papers to grade "because it's good for you," and it's hardly fair to expect the student to do something you wouldn't dream of doing yourself.

The more imaginative or unusual the assignment, alas, the greater the likelihood it won't be done. "Examine the bones in the meat your mother cooks for dinner tonight and be prepared to report tomorrow on the cell structure," will harvest a crop of students who had chili, meat loaf, or hot dogs for dinner. Exercises in the textbook or exercises run off on the spirit duplicator will stand a better chance of being turned in completed.

Give a specific assignment. When a teacher says, "Read as much as you feel you need to read to be able to discuss this topic on a panel tomorrow," three-fourths of his students will surreptitiously write "none" in their assignment notebooks.

Take the school calendar into account. If there's a basketball tournament coming up, ease up on the homework assignments. Be sure the students understand you are taking their

convenience into account in this way. A considerate teacher will get more work out of the students in the long run.

Be prepared to cope with cheating on homework assignments. Mom or dad may do the work for the student at home, of course; but more common will be the significant percentage of students who "get their homework" fifteen minutes before class by borrowing and copying the paper of some accommodating drudge who's already done the dog work. A simple check of error patterns won't necessarily apprehend the culprits, either. Culprits are smarter than they used to be; nowadays, they change a few of the answers.

Student Teams

A situation may arise in which you wish to form your students into teams for debates or a series of skits. By and large, group work of this kind will go better if you assign team members on a basis of personality pattern rather than scholastic ability. One aggressive, one submissive, and three average personality types make a good working team. If you place two or more aggressive students on the same team, you'll spend your time breaking up squabbles; if you allow too many passive types on one team, it won't accomplish anything.

In such group work, avoid the mistake of awarding one grade to an entire team on the basis of its group performance. Two or three members of the team will do most of the work and, in fairness, deserve better marks than their teammates. Make the group performance *part* of the individual grade, if you like, but not all of it. It will be your task to maintain surveillance of each group to be sure you know which students are working and which aren't, and award individual marks accordingly.

Maintaining such groups in operation over an entire school year may be both pleasurable and instructionally profitable for the teams whose members get along well together, but the reverse will be true of the others. It's a better policy to keep rotating the members.

Standardized Tests

In nearly all high schools nowadays, it is the counselors who attend to the school's formal testing program. However, you may be asked to help administer tests in connection with curriculum projects, or to evaluate new materials or techniques. There are several points to keep in mind:

1. Standardized paper-and-pencil tests give approximations, and that's all. Reading teachers, for example, can't expect to place students who score 8th-grade level on a standardized reading test in an 8th-grade book, although

nearly all the 8th-grade scorers will end up in the 7 to 9 range. These tests aren't nearly as valuable for individual measurement as they are for group measurement. In a larger sample, individual errors tend to cancel themselves out.

2. If you're due to give a standardized test, take the test manual home and study it the night before. Get together whatever you need ahead of time—answer cards, a stop watch, pencils, etc.

3. Everything about a standardized test is standardized, including the instructions the teacher gives the students who take it. If the manual tells you it's all right to explain, explain; if not, don't. Say what the manual tells you to say and *only* what the manual tells you to say. (Yes, I know it sounds stiff and formal; but say it anyway. The test data will be inaccurate if you extemporize.) Be a persnickety timekeeper. Insist that students who finish early be quiet so the others can work in peace.

4. Don't talk while the students are taking the test. If a student has a question, go to his seat and whisper.

5. Most tests will have sample items to show the students how to mark their answers. No matter how loudly your students may groan, "Aw, we know how to do this," take them through the sample-marking business anyway. There will be transfers from other schools who won't be familiar with your answer forms, or timid types who have forgotten.

Grading

If the conversation languishes in the faculty lounge someday at noon, try launching a discussion of grading philosophies—just for the fun of watching the sparks fly. No two people will agree, and you will find as many interpretations of the school's stated policy on the subject as there are teachers.

In your training courses, you doubtless covered this logicdefying question rather thoroughly and are already familiar with the paradoxes, inequities, and plain tomfooleries implicit in the issue. At any rate, nothing is to be gained here by punching at the hornet's nest, beyond suggesting a line of defense that you might find valuable in warding off outraged students at report card time.

Obviously, grading always was, is, and will be controlled by the teacher. The students are at a disadvantage. They must play the game according to rules that remain the same, year in and year out. It is the teacher who may raise or lower the net, mark off the court, schedule the matches, and specify the kind of rackets and balls that will be used. If the teacher wants to produce a batch of good grades to encourage a dispirited class, he lowers the net and gives an easy test, or gives a hard test that he "grades easy." He can penalize the members of a slow class by scheduling an uneven match— he can give them the same test he gives his brighter students and allot grades to both classes according to the same scale. He can arbitrarily establish a cutoff point, curve or no curve, and flunk everybody below that.

At this point, you may protest that the problem has a simple solution. The teacher should simply give everyone a fair shake. But it is one of the built-in ironies of grading that the teacher *can't* give everyone a fair shake. One student coasts along, yet makes the best scores in the class. Will you flunk him because he coasts? Another student works like a demon and still makes the lowest scores in the class. Will you give him an A for the effort he has expended? Your problem is to decide how you can manage your gradebook so that you cheat the fewest number of students the least frequently.

Curiously enough, high school students seldom notice, or even care, if you've raised or lowered the net or given them a shorter or longer court. They feel it is your privilege as a teacher to set the game up to suit yourself, even though the way you set it up may be chopping them off at the knees. But once the points have been earned and have gone into the gradebook, they are sensitive almost to the point of paranoia about honest dealing in the way the teacher averages out those points for final grades. Never "give" quarter and semester grades, "compute" them. If an indignant student

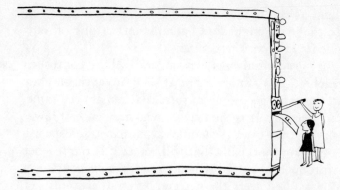

doesn't believe he really made the D you put on his report card, refigure his grade while he watches you. Ask him to check your figures. If you find your first grade was wrong, correct it on the gradebook, the report card, and the transcript, even if the incorrect grade was in his favor and the new, corrected mark is F!

Make it known that a student may have a list of his grades any time during the semester—as long as he doesn't interrupt class proceedings to obtain them. He may come by your desk before or after class, or before or after school.

It's not a good plan to teach an entire six- or nine-week period and post no more than two or three sets of grades on which to base your report card marks. From the standpoint of good instruction, this meager sample of a student's work doesn't give you a proper indication of how well he's learning; neither is it serving you as a proper guide for your presentation of new material. From the standpoint of sound practice in awarding marks, you haven't given the student a fair chance to show what he can do. One grade a week should provide a minimum sample to provide the data for computing report card marks. Two grades per week would be better.

Many schools send out notices midway through the grading period to warn parents when their child is failing a subject (*see* Deficiency Notices, page 78). Whether notices are sent to parents or not, experienced teachers like to run a speculative eye over the gradebook every two weeks or so to determine which students are courting failure. They talk to those students privately and give them fair warning about their status.

Grading Reports, Papers, and Themes

The first time you face a foot-high stack of student reports, research papers, or themes, and realize they are yours, all yours, to wade through somehow, your eyes may glaze over and you may begin work on them feeling somewhat like Hercules in the Augean stable. With constructive planning, however, you can make the experience of checking those reports valuable, and maybe even exciting.

Jot down a checklist of points you emphasized with your students while the reports were in preparation. Arrange these points as column heads across a sheet of ruled paper (one sheet for each class). At the far right, have a column for the grades on the reports. At the top of the sheet, make a note of the date and nature of the assignment. Down the left-hand side of the sheet, leave space for the names of students. (You might want to run off a number of these forms on the spirit duplicator.)

Grade each point as it has been covered by each student by putting a score in the corresponding column. If you like, work out a system for weighting some points more heavily than others. Go through the entire stack of reports once before deciding on any grades you will put in the grades column. This way, you can gauge the over-all quality of the class' work better and be more equitable in judging which students deserve higher marks than others.

Don't throw your checklist sheets away after you have posted the grades in your gradebook. File them. You can use the list of points as your teaching objectives when you repeat the assignment next year. You will also need the filled-in sheets for comparing student progress the next time you assign similar reports. More valuable still, checklists make good day-to-day teaching guides, for, by analyzing your students' scoring on points you have emphasized, you will discover where you must strengthen your daily class work. If your class load is low enough to permit work with individual students, you may be able to follow up on some of the more glaring weaknesses that turn up.

Grading Daily Drills and Exercises

Don't check every daily drill and exercise. You don't need to. Take the stack of exercises that has been turned in for the day and go through it and remove every third paper. So you're due at a meeting in thirty minutes? In that case, remove every fifth paper. Check those. Convert the scores to grades and post the grades to your gradebook. Next day, return the papers you checked to the proper students and collect the next stack. Treat them the same way, and so on.

Over a month or two, you will find an accumulation of grades for some students and none for others. Abandon your random selection technique for a few days and equalize your sample for the students you seem to have missed.

Don't make the mistake of making your random selection while the students are there with you in class and all eyes are on you. In other words, don't let it become a matter for student quibbling: "Please check mine this time, Mr. Jones"; "You checked mine three times in a row, and that's not fair." Selection is your business. Take up all the papers, every time. Keep them guessing.

Vary the procedure occasionally. You might, for instance, check only items ten through twenty of a thirty-item exercise. But in this situation, check each paper, not every third one.

Having students exchange papers and check them while in class saves time and, more valuable, gives the student quicker knowledge of results. Some classes will be able to check their own papers and learn something from the experience, but when you try this, be on the lookout for wholesale cheating if the students think the scores will be entered in your gradebook, or wholesale indifference if they believe they won't be.

From the standpoint of learning gains, having students check their own papers all the time, every time, is most valuable of all. When the student merely scrutinizes his own test paper with the teacher's (or another student's) red checks to indicate his mistakes, he learns what he got wrong; but he may or may not go to the trouble of finding out the right answers. It's an educational tragedy that cheating among students is so widespread in so many schools, that having students check their own papers all the time, every time, results in almost no learning gains at all. In fact, one of the benefits of individualizing all the instruction in your classes is that you can have the student check his own work from an answer key at your desk, where you can breathe down his neck to keep him from changing his answers or marking his errors as correct answers.

Test Formats and Grading

By thinking through your testing procedures ahead of time, you can work out tests and exercises that require less clerical time to check, waste less paper (rationed in some schools), and are of better quality as far as evaluation is concerned. Suppose, for example, you are trying to find out if your students have learned basic algebraic processes. You type up your test items as follows:

1. In the formula $A = 2 S^2 - LW$, find A if $S = 10$, $L = 4$, and $W = 2$. _____

2. If $a = 2$ and $b = -4$, then $3 a(a+b)$ equals _____

The student must work out the problems on an auxiliary worksheet and then write in his answers. To check a test like this, you must read each answer. Sometimes the answers will look more like Egyptian hieroglyphics than Arabic numerals. Decoding them will take far more time than is

necessary to find out what you want to know, which is whether your students have learned basic algebraic processes.

Now suppose you type up your test items as multiple-choice questions, like this:

1. In the formula $A = 2 S^2 - LW$, find A if $S = 10, L = 4$, and $W = 2$.

    (a) 392   (b) 208   (c) 102   (d) 32   (e) none of these

2. If $a = 2$ and $b = -4$, then $3 a(a+b)$ equals

    (a) -48   (b) -12   (c) +12   (d) +36   (e) none of these

If you require the student to circle or check the correct answer, you avoid the hieroglyphic hang-up. There is no need to figure out what the student intended to indicate as the correct answer. However, with the items typed as they are in this example, you must still scan each item on each test paper to discover if the right answers have been circled or checked.

There is a third way:

1. In the formula $A = 2 S^2 - LW$, find A if $S = 10, L = 4$, and $W = 2$.

    (a) 392 (b) 208 (c) 102 (d) 32 (e) none   (a)(b)(c)(d)(e)

2. If $a = 2$ and $b = -4$, then $3 a(a + b)$ equals

    (a) -48 (b) -12 (c) +12 (d) +36 (e) none   (a)(b)(c)(d)(e)

To make a key for checking a test drawn up in this format, take the test yourself, marking the correct answers. Then cut the answer strip from the right side of one of your test papers and punch a hole where each correct answer occurs (you can borrow a handpunch from the office). Lay the punched answer strip over a student's paper; correct answers are visible instantly. It should take you no more than two seconds per test page to mark incorrect answers and jot down the number wrong.

The secret of good multiple-choice tests, as you may already have discovered for yourself from taking objective tests in high school and college, is in the test maker's choice of wrong answers. Compare the distractors in the two questions below:

> Steve Canyon is a (1) kind of automobile, (2) geographical location, (3) planet, (4) comic strip character.
>
> Steve Canyon is a (1) cartoonist, (2) TV hero, (3) comic strip character, (4) newspaper columnist.

The closer your distractors come to the incorrect answers your students really might give, the more sensitive they will be in testing what your students know.

For speedier checking, set up true-false items, like this:

> Genghis Khan was of Polynesian descent.   (T)   (F)

Avoid the adjectives "most," "none," and "all," which are usually dead giveaways that the statement is false.

Sometimes you find teachers who object to multiple-choice tests on the ground that students shouldn't be checking A, B, C, or D if they cannot write their numbers (or letters, sentences, or paragraphs) legibly; they should be practicing writing their numbers. These teachers are right; the students do need such practice. But is a test or drill of this kind the best place for them to practice? If the teacher can't decipher a student's answer on this exercise, how will he ever know if the student did or did not know how to solve the problem? The teacher would be attempting to evaluate two different skills, not just one; and the inability of the student to perform one skill, penmanship, would interfere with the teacher's finding out if he had mastered the other skill, finding correct answers to the algebra problems. If you're interested in evaluating your students on penmanship, require them to turn in their worksheets for the test. By glancing over the worksheets, you can give the students a separate penmanship grade, which will make more sense both to them and to you—and you'll still save time.

A set of mathematics drills and tests won't require an alarming amount of paper, even for three or four classes. However, a literature or social studies examination can run up to ten pages if the masters are prepared on a pica type-

writer and double spaced, as they should be for easiest
reading. A ten-page literature examination for 125 students
may consume your entire paper allowance for the year. To

get around this, furnish students with an answer sheet
separate from the test paper. Use the test papers themselves
over and over. You will only need 35 or 40 copies of the test
itself, because you will use the same set many times. However, you will need as many answer sheets as there are
students. Since you may be able to get two answer sheets
out of one sheet of paper, you have cut your paper requirement by almost two-thirds.

Mechanical Grading

During the first week of school, find out if your school
district has an automatic test-grading machine teachers may
use. Since this is your first year, within the next nine months
you will be constructing tests and exercises that you may
still be using, with modifications, ten years from now. If you
construct these first tests and drills to follow a multiple-
choice or true-false format, which is a requirement of
mechanical grading, your students may enter their answers
on mark sense cards as well as on your homemade answer
sheets. Machine grading can save a fantastic number of
clerical man-hours, man-hours that you can use for teaching
in the years to come.

If your school district has an automatic grading device, find out where the machine is located and what kind of reaction time you can expect. There may be no difficulty in securing time on the machine, but you may experience delay in securing the time of the technician who operates it. If you are able to get cards back within a day, and if it doesn't take you more than fifteen minutes to get to the machine and back, you've got a good thing going for you.

Machine grading will be excellent in situations where you are teaching three or more sections of the same class and plan to administer either the same test or a similar version of the same test on the same days. In short, machine grading is good for big or long-term jobs. For one class only, it isn't much help unless the machine is in your own building and you can stroll in, obtain the immediate services of the technician, get your cards checked, and be out again in ten minutes. With a punched answer strip, you can check one class set of cards or papers by hand in the same length of time without leaving your classroom. (In the next few years, you may have your own grading device, the size of a shoe box, clamped to the side of your desk. Until then, keep reminding your principal so he won't forget you want one.)

Lay Readers, Monitors, and Teachers' Aides

For some reason that apparently has nothing to do with Christian Science, the term "lay reader" has become accepted pedagese for those college students, housewives, or retired teachers hired by a school district to grade English themes. Use of such personnel is becoming increasingly widespread. Although the lay reader is usually retained for the use of English teachers only, there is no reason why history, science or journalism teachers couldn't share in this service if they pulled the right strings. Every little bit helps.

The clever teacher will customize the lay reader's work. While posting marks to his gradebook from the bundle of themes the lay reader has checked, the teacher may glance over the student's errors and write a personal note of some kind on his paper: "Spelling has improved this time" or "A good job—congratulations."

Teachers with hundred-plus pupil loads will have to use student help of some kind in the classroom if they're to function at all. Student monitors can attend to housekeeping tasks, such as straightening and organizing bookcase materials, putting away maps and lab equipment, and erasing and cleaning the chalkboard. With the proper training, student monitors can perform as media technicians in charge of setting up and operating tape recorders and motion picture and filmstrip projectors. They can check single-answer tests and exercises and post grades or raw scores to your gradebook. They can check roll and take care of the procedure for reporting absences to the office. If it's a bulletin board you want, supply a diagram and the necessary letters and pictures. Don't entrust student monitors with anything too tricky.

The new teacher should wait until he knows his students well before he makes permanent assignments for student monitor tasks. The student who seems reliable the first day of school often turns out to be all blow and no show. In choosing students to help you, brains won't be as valuable as thoroughness, a desire to be helpful, and the ability to assume responsibility. Don't choose one student in each class, choose two or three and rotate them. In assisting with classroom chores, the student will necessarily lose the benefit of classroom instruction. By rotating a team of students, you don't penalize any one of them too much in this respect.

At the outset, try to get all of your student monitors to come for a couple of thirty-minute training sessions before or after school. Teach this little class exactly as you would your regular classes. Demonstrate the tasks that need to be done. Let them practice doing them; give the members of the group several test papers and have them do the checking while you supervise.

In some schools, work-study programs or service clubs provide incentive for this kind of work by means of wages, service pins, or other recognition. Without rewards, you will

find a few of your student monitors losing interest as the novelty wears off. Even with rewards, you will find a few who aren't able to do the work. Replace them tactfully. Give them a chance to resign. Ask your remaining monitors to train the replacement just as you trained them ("each one teach one"); supervise the training procedure from a back seat.

In classes of unusually hostile students, you may not be able to recruit student monitors. Students who served in this capacity would be ridiculed by their classmates. When this happens, don't designate any students as official monitors; call on different class members to perform simple tasks from time to time. They can pass out books, straighten shelves, put the projector and screen in place (although you will actually operate the machine), and return papers that have been checked.

Your classroom assistant may not be a student at all, but an adult whose salary is paid by the school district, a teacher's aide. This doesn't alter your obligation to train the person and maintain supervision to be sure the work is done properly. Let your teacher's aide begin with a few responsibilities. As she learns to do them well, add others, demonstrating techniques and methods as you go. Don't dump a ton of complicated details on her at the beginning and then complain because she's inefficient. She'll be no better than you train her to be.

*Discipline**

The best time-saver for any teacher of any subject is to establish control of student behavior in the classroom as soon as possible. True, paper work gobbles up class time; but the most voracious time-gobbler of all is a room full of rambunctious adolescents who resist settling down to learn. Your first year will be more difficult in this respect because the students won't know you. Maintain close communication with the vice-principal and the dean of boys and the dean of girls. Put yourself in the hands of these discipline experts and follow their advice in dealing with difficult students.

*For a thorough discussion of this problem, *see* Jenny Gray, *The Teacher's Survival Guide*, Palo Alto, Calif.: Fearon Publishers, Inc., 1967.

three

Records, Reports, and Forms

School personnel are concerned with maintenance and control of information, objects, and people. The point of the educational game is to get the information (curriculum content) into the people (students) with the support and assistance of objects (buildings, desks, chalk, duplicator masters, textbooks, trampolines, brooms, Bunsen's burners—you name it). In order to maintain and control these three things so they are properly juxtaposed to perform their basic function, school personnel must communicate with one another. Forms of various kinds make it easier.

Most of the paper work for which you will be responsible will have to do with attendance, computation and reporting of grades, noncurricular student supervision, scheduling, and referrals, all of which fall within the general area of student control. You will spend a minimum of three hours a day doing things about student control. You will read announcements or see to it that they are read. You will move a talkative student and change the seating chart. From time to time, you will meet with student clubs and walk a beat in the hall. Of the three hours, a minimum of one hour per day will be spent dealing with information about student control. You will record this information and share it via forms, records, and reports with other members of the staff.

Attendance

Sometime, somewhere, when you least expect it, someone will say, "Smile! We're going to audit your school's attendance records!" Although it won't be you, personally, but the people in the attendance office who will bear the physical brunt of such an audit, it will definitely be *your* data they will scrutinize so carefully. (It isn't that the auditors are all that interested in the little people; what they're interested in is the ADA money the state is paying your district on the basis of how many little people you claim show up in your homeroom every day.)

Although there are as many different methods of keeping attendance records as there are schools, from the standpoint of the teacher, they will nearly all break down into two operations: (1) daily reporting of attendance, which every teacher will surely do, and (2) weekly or monthly preparation of the permanent record, which might be done in the office rather than by the teacher. Customarily, the main purpose of the homeroom is to get the daily student count from which the permanent attendance record is prepared later. Teachers in your school may have a special book in which attendance for the homeroom roster is kept, or you may set aside one section of your gradebook for this purpose. We're talking now about the record *you* keep, you understand. There will be another standard form, or packs of student cards, for reporting your homeroom attendance to the office.

In order to get an accurate count every day during the homeroom period, you will have to train students in your homeroom to report to you *before* they go to the emergency student senate hearing, to other homerooms to drum up business for Saturday's car wash, or to the home economics room to sew up a ripped skirt. Discourage message bearers— "Marilyn said to tell you . . . ." If you don't insist that

Marilyn show up in person, you'll soon find yourself checking homeroom attendance entirely via messenger, which is not a very businesslike way to do it. If you explain to your homeroom students why their presence is necessary and what the procedure means to the school, you will have better cooperation in this endeavor.

Your teachers' handbook will tell you if teachers in your school are responsible for maintaining permanent records for their homerooms. If this chore is handled in the attendance office, not by you, offer up a quick prayer of thanksgiving. If the job is yours, well . . . .

Procedure at your school may require that the permanent attendance record be brought up to date and turned in to the office once a week, once a month, or at the end of each grading period. If each student in your homeroom could be depended upon to enroll the first day of school and stay enrolled until the last day of school, the permanent attendance record could be taken care of simply and quickly. However, if your school is plagued by large numbers of late enrollments, transfers, dropouts, flunkouts, and blithe spirits who simply walk out the front gate never to return, the task is not so simple; it's more like trying to reweave a window screen that tried to stop a double load of buckshot.

For each of your thirty-odd homeroom students, you will have to copy the line of absences from your roll book, chicken scratch for chicken scratch. The dates must correspond—not roughly, but exactly. You will also record date of enrollment, date of termination, and total days present plus total days absent (which must tally with total days enrolled, leaving out school holidays). All of this must balance out. Your total horizontal chicken scratches for individual students must equal your total vertical chicken scratches for each day. In addition, you will need a code entry to show reason for termination (transfer, disciplinary, illness, etc.) and, possibly, the number of tardies as well.

By all means, arrange to sit in with an experienced teacher in your school the first two or three times you undertake this procedure so there will be someone to answer your questions. Don't take these records home with you to work on. They are irreplaceable. If your apartment building burned down, you'd be in an odd spot, indeed.

Always make your entries in pencil first and ink them in later. Arm yourself with a regular fountain pen (ballpoint won't erase), a bottle of ink of the prescribed color, and a vial of chlorine bleach and toothpicks for making ink erasures in very small spaces. Even after you ink in your entries and turn the monster in at the office, some helpful soul down there is liable to point out a mistaken entry or termination date, which means you must change totals both horizontally and vertically.

Class Records

Every native-born American knows a teacher's class record book, or gradebook, when he sees one. Elementary, secondary, and college teachers have used them for half a century. They are nine inches long by five inches wide, have brown fiberboard covers, and are spiral bound. They are usually studded with paper clips or trussed with rubber bands to permit quick access to frequently-used pages. In September, the book is virginal and crisply noncommittal. By January, the battered covers embrace not only grades, but an assortment of student papers, notes for future lesson plans, and the agenda from last month's faculty meeting. By June, when the grades have at last been delivered, the papers returned, and the lessons taught, it is flat once more—

a coffee-ringed, pulpy husk, doomed to temporary interment in the crypt reserved for the school's inactive records before it is ultimately cremated.

Newer styles in record books have appeared on the market in recent years. They are bigger and provide loose-leaf pages for lesson plans as well as grades. Best of all, leather bindings and larger size allow the teacher to pack up to ten class sets of student papers, which in itself rates several points over the old, narrow model.

Let's hope that record books are on their way out. In the near future, at least a few schools may be equipped with central computers where all grade and attendance data are stored. Input and readout stations would be installed at teachers' desks, counselors' and administrators' offices, teachers' workrooms, etc. The present cost of initial installation for an eighty-classroom school is about a million dollars. Another possibility is an individual, portable, computerized record book. This is a miniaturized information storage and retrieval system about the size and weight of one of your classroom dictionaries. It will store your class rosters, plus attendance and grades for each student. By attaching a readout mechanism, you may have a printed record, with averaged grades, whenever you choose. Being transferred to another school? Take your record book with you. The present cost of this device is about ten thousand dollars.

Inside the covers of either the old- or new-style record book, there are several full-width pages for listing your students, class by class, and narrower pages of printed grids, in the little squares of which you will place thousands upon thousands of little marks before the year is over. Horizontal lines are for the student; vertical lines are for the school day. A diagonal line from the upper right-hand to the lower left-hand corner of a given square almost universally means the student was absent on that particular day. Beyond that, you will mark absences, tardies, or daily grades in your school's, or your own, private code.

Your class record book will serve as ancillary brain and conscience for the coming year; it will serve you well if you keep it in an orderly way. Your class record tells you whether your class generally and individual students particularly are making progress. Your entries should convey accurate information; you must be able to determine what work to have students make up after absences; you must be able to talk intelligently to parents about what their son or daughter has achieved; and, of course, you will compute quarter and semester marks from daily work and from test grades you have recorded. Semester marks are the ones that will become part of the student's permanent transcript and will determine such important things as whether or not he is accepted for the college of his choice.

If possible, you will keep your class rosters in alphabetical order, because it's easier for you to find individual names that way. It is seldom possible to keep your rosters alphabetized very long, for you will add, drop, and sometimes re-enroll students as the school year progresses. To drop a student, fill in the block on the grid to indicate his termination date and fill in his line on your record book with colored pencil. If you do this lightly, his grades will still be visible should you need them again. To add a student, add his name below the others on your roster and fill in the block on the grid to indicate the enrollment date.

Some teachers keep percentage grades, some keep points, and some prefer letter grades. Percentages require that raw scores on daily work and tests be converted to a 100-point scale and then averaged to a letter grade for reporting on report cards. Letters must be converted to number values for totaling or averaging and back to letters again for reporting. Points (raw scores) are the simplest of the three, because at grading time they require only totaling and one conversion to a letter grade. A disadvantage of the point system is that raw scores don't mean much unless compared with other raw scores. It's difficult to tell a student, in any significant way, how well he did on a given assignment. Another disadvantage is that the test or quiz with the most items automatically becomes the most important of the year, unless the teacher maintains a strategy of doubling, tripling, or halving the points allowed to achieve an appropriate weighting. Both letters and points require less space than percentages.

To be ready with an answer for the student who wants to know what he made on the map exercise last month, for the parents at an interview, and for the student who has been absent and must make up work, turn your book sideways and jot down in the vertical space for that day what the grades are for. This may be in your own shorthand—"lab proj 16," "sp qu 103," "wk tst."

Grades for work done by individual students, but not by the class, pose a problem. You have given Jim some remedial exercises to do and he has completed the work promptly and carefully. You want to give him credit for it. How to make the entry? One solution is to code these grades by entering them with colored pencils.

Another excellent use for colored pencils is to code grade values. For example, you may want oral reports to count twice as much as weekly lab exercises; enter oral report grades in green pencil. Vocabulary test scores might be in blue, the final exam in orange.

Absences and "Tardies"

Some schools require teachers to list absences for each class on a special form provided for the purpose. The "absence slips" are either sent to the office by student messenger every period or are clipped on the classroom door to be picked up by an office girl.

Because there are so many slips and forms of this kind to be signed during the ordinary school day, you may wonder if it would be worthwhile to have a rubber stamp of your signature made. It probably isn't. On most forms, your

initials or hastily-written last name will suffice, and this only takes a couple of seconds. To use a rubber stamp, you must have a flat surface under the paper to be stamped. You'll also need a stamp pad whose lid must be kept closed to keep it from drying out. A rubber stamp, moreover, won't work for forms that must be signed in triplicate. Also, it can be swiped.

If your school is typical, there will be an elaborate and, alas, necessary rigmarole about admit-to-class slips after the student has been absent. It goes like this: (1) Student returns to school after absence, (2) student must present note from parent or doctor to personnel in attendance office so that he may be issued a form by the attendance secretary to admit him to class, and (3) teachers sign this slip as the student meets successive classes during his first day back in school. If the absence has been for an acceptable reason—illness, medical treatment, etc.—the admit slip will show the student to be "excused," in which case he may make up work he has missed. If, on the other hand, he went fishing or was detained in the juvenile home, the absence will be "unexcused" and he may not make up the work he missed.

In some schools, the only "excused" and "unexcused" categories the office worries about are the ones affecting the ADA allowance, and teachers are expected to use their own judgment in allowing students to make up work they have missed. Indicate in your record book if absences are excused or unexcused.

There may also be slips showing excused and unexcused "tardies." Sometimes teachers are instructed to dispose of these in some way—to turn them in to the attendance officer or to the homeroom teacher, for example. Your handbook will tell you.

There will be a procedure to take care of students who are present in school but fail to appear in your class ("cuts"). If your absences are sent to the office period by period, the dean of boys or the dean of girls will take care of the matter without any further paper transactions on your part. If there is no period-by-period reporting of absences, you will assume the responsibility for reporting or disciplining your own cuts. Each teacher will be issued a list of students reported absent from homerooms. From this daily list of students absent from school, you will be able to determine which students were present in school but absent from your classes. Then you will either report cuts to the dean of boys or the dean of girls on a form provided for the purpose, or, if it is expected of you, initiate your own disciplinary action.

Class Count Forms

At the beginning of the school year, all teachers in your school may be asked to fill out class count forms every day. This is a printed report on which you enter the number of students in your homeroom and what classes you teach during which periods and how many students there are in each of these classes. During the first two weeks of school, your administrators will be registering new students daily, and it is the class count information from teachers that enables them to avoid overloading classes. After the registration rush subsides, you will be asked for class counts less frequently. If your school is being scheduled by computer, you shouldn't have to bother with this operation at all.

Program Changes and Drops

Occasionally a student is inadvertently scheduled into the wrong class, or a teacher may feel that a student is so far above or so far below his classmates that a change should be made in that student's program. Whether you are dropping him as an old student or acquiring him as a new student, you will be asked to sign a program change form. As much as anything else, this procedure represents a courtesy to the teacher; it officially notifies the teacher ahead of time that a student is coming, and gives him an opportunity to issue textbooks and otherwise orient the new student. Experienced teachers make the change in their record books immediately. There have been cases where such entries were overlooked and the student existed in limbo for several months although he was physically present in class every day.

In much the same way, you will be expected to sign a clearance sheet and give a terminal grade to students leaving school. Before the student is finally cleared, he must turn in his books, gym equipment, locks for both gym and hall lockers, and so on. You must indicate by your signature on a form that he has cleared with you on this score. The form will be placed in your box or will be brought around by an office girl. Record the matter in your record book immediately.

Reporting Grades

Getting grades ready to report is far more time-consuming than actually posting the marks to the report card or permanent record forms. There are cardboard or plastic "grade averagers" on the market to help teachers with marking period chores. They cost anywhere from fifty cents to five dollars, and perform varying quantities of the grade computing operation, depending on the price. They are advertised in professional journals for ordering by mail, and are available in college bookstores and through school supply houses.

Lacking a "grade averager," ask about borrowing an adding machine from your school's business education department. You can probably arrange to sign one out overnight or for the week end.

If you have a good head for figures, you may arrive at your grade averages by a system of canceling out A-F and B-D combinations, which you then count as C's, and averaging the remainder either up or down. When there aren't many grades to average, this is easy and works quite well. If you have more than eight grades to average, an adding machine will be quicker.

Decide ahead of time how you will weight your test, theme, or report grades, and then be consistent with the weighting pattern in computing grades for each student. If you have quiz grades that you wish to make equal to three times the value of daily grades, count the quiz grades three times instead of once. Marks for important reports and final exams will be averaged in after you have found the average of the daily grades.

Work with a straightedge, a ruler, or a piece of folded paper to keep your eye traveling along each student's line of marks. Be careful that you don't find yourself computing grades from the line above and the line below, a maneuver that won't give you very accurate grade averages.

Some schools have two nine-week grading periods per semester. Teachers in such systems must develop a policy for arriving at one semester mark from these two nine-week periods that will be fair both to the student and to the college or employer that will one day be deciding whether to accept the student's application. Ordinarily, an A and a C will average to a B, and cause no trouble. However, if the student earns a B the first quarter and a C the second, what do you do? The most common practice seems to lean to the last grade as being the better long-term indicator of the student's strength in the subject. A C or a C+ might be the more stable grade. A first-quarter D and a second-quarter A would be better at a B or B– than a C or C+.

After reading the preceeding paragraphs, you may begin to understand why experienced teachers plan their lessons so there will be a minimum of clerical work the last week of the grading period. They have their hands full preparing their grades during this time. They start to work on them early and make the last test as easy to check as possible.

There are two things that will happen to grades you compute for students in your classes: (1) They are reported to parents, with copies usually going to counselors and the dean of boys and the dean of girls; and (2) they become part of the students' permanent records in the school and are available to colleges and prospective employers, including the military. In addition to the permanent record of attendance discussed previously, there will be a permanent 9″ x 5″ record card or a folder, or both, for each student; it will follow him through the grades in your school district. Methods of maintaining these records will differ from system to system. The records may be kept electronically, or the necessary entries may be made by the counselors or other office personnel in your school. In some schools, they will be brought up to date by homeroom teachers. You will be given careful instructions on how to post these records. As in the case of permanent attendance records, they must be in ink and they must be accurate.

In some schools, report card grades from teachers are redistributed to individual student report cards by computers in the district office, and the cards are mailed from there to parents. From the teacher's point of view, the only thing that changes in this kind of operation is that he probably won't be responsible for maintaining permanent record cards. Procedure for computation of individual student grades remains the same. For the teacher, reporting grades electronically simply means "bubbling" mark sense cards instead of marking permanent records or marking student rosters for other teachers. It works this way: The teacher is given a deck of mark sense cards for each of his classes. Each card will have the name of the student printed on it. The teacher will fill in the proper "bubble" to indicate the grade. You may also have a pack of cards for your homeroom on which you will be required to enter attendance data for permanent records. This means you will fill in the number of days in attendance, date of enrollment or drop, and, perhaps, reason for termination.

Deficiency Notices

Many schools follow a policy (which pays off in improved home-school relations, by the way) of prereporting to parents if failure of a student is imminent. This gives the parent an opportunity to apply pressure at home to avert disaster. True, parents don't always apply the pressure; but at least they have been given the opportunity, and the ugly surprise of that F on the report card has been dulled.

"Snitch notices," as the kids call them, are usually made out by teachers midway through the grading period. They are made out in triplicate or quadruplicate; one copy is mailed to the parent, one goes to the counselor, one goes to the homeroom teacher or dean, and one copy is retained by the teacher. Read your handbook carefully to determine which students should be reported. If you are reporting both F and D averages, you will have a larger task on your hands than if you are reporting F students only. Very little grade averaging will be required to see which students are failing; there will be nothing but a long line of F's. In your gradebook, be sure to code-mark students you have reported deficient.

Referrals

There should be laws of pedagogy as there are laws of physics. For openers, I herewith submit Gray's First Law: The bigger the school, the longer the form. If you are teaching in a little institution with two hundred students, you may send a pupil who becomes ill to the nurse immediately. If there are eight hundred students in the school, it may be necessary to have the student wait a moment while you fill out a brief referral slip and sign your name. If the school numbers eighteen hundred students or more, the kid may pass out on the floor as you fill in "Name of parent or guardian," "Home telephone number," "Reason for referral," "Has student suffered similar attacks in the classroom before," and so on, through several inches of fine print.

The same situation seems to hold true for referrals to the counselor, the dean of boys or the dean of girls, and the school psychologist or welfare worker. When you begin teaching, you will be given blank forms for such referrals. Study them carefully and keep a place in your file where you will be able to get at the form you need in a hurry.

The Exceptions

What will turn you, yourself, into a case for referral to the school psychologist is to expend considerable time and effort with your handbook and the mountain of forms and blanks to familiarize yourself with school procedures, only to find yourself the butt of a school-wide joke when you do things the way the book says. ("But, my dear, we haven't done it *that* way for *years!*")

Fortunately, exceptions to the printed procedural directives are, themselves, an exception to the rule for schools. The teachers' handbook exists to enable teachers to perform their duties properly, and the school district will be rare that subverts its own best interests in this way. Few of them will knowingly allow erroneous instructions to remain in the handbook. As a precaution, though, the new teacher shouldn't plunge into a lengthy session of record-keeping with only his handbook to guide him. Check with a teacher who has taught in the district for several years. ("The handbook says so-and-so. Is this *really* the way you do it?")

Audio-visual Requirements

In the category of logistics, the amount of paper work required will also depend on school and district size. If there are four history teachers in the district's lone high school, the history teacher may send a student with a note to the classroom of the department head to pick up a map of Cambodia for use five minutes later. But if there are twenty-five teachers in the history department of one of the district's fourteen high schools, five minutes lead time is scarcely sufficient. The mapless teacher will need to prepare a check-out slip in duplicate to obtain the item from his own school's department office, or a requisition slip in triplicate or quadruplicate to get it from the district's audio-visual center. Anywhere from two days to two weeks may transpire before he claims the item or receives notification that it isn't available.

Orders for projection materials and equipment are subject to the same contingencies; so are tapes, study prints, models, and such specialized reading equipment as pacers and tachistoscopes.

Library

Obtaining books from the library requires no special check-out procedure, unless you wish to retain the library books in your classroom beyond the usual time limit for book loans. In that case, there may be a special form the librarian will have you use for check-out. There may also be special forms for reference works that are not ordinarily checked out of the library at all.

Want to take your class to the library to do research work? Ask the librarian about the procedure. There may be a form, or you may be asked to sign the librarian's log for the dates and periods you wish.

Textbook Issue

There will probably be a form for textbooks that are turned over to you for issue to the students. Each textbook will

carry its own number. The form will call for your name, the
date, the classroom number, the quantity of books, the con-
dition of the books (new, good, medium, poor), and the
numbers born by the texts themselves. When you pick up
your students' textbooks, try to get a series of books num-
bered consecutively, from 500 to 600, for example. Book-
keeping, both for you and for the office, is easier with a
hundred consecutive numbers than with a hundred scrambled
ones, each of which must be listed separately. The school
will usually provide class sheets or student cards on which
will be entered the date of issue, the title and number of
the book, and the student's signature. Accuracy is highly
recommended. You and you alone are responsible for these
books.

Locks and Lockers

Sheets or cards for checking out locks and assigning hall
lockers to your homeroom students will resemble those used
to check out textbooks. Again, consecutive numbers will
be more convenient. Students will also sign for locks, either
on your master sheet or on their cards, which they leave
with you.

Everything checked out at the beginning of the year must
be checked back in at the end of the year, whether you check
it out from someone else or someone else checks it out from
you. Keep this happy thought in the back of your mind
when you are tempted to cut corners with your paper work.
Who'll suffer in June from your sloppy September records?
You will.

Room Inventory

June will also bring with it a frenetic exercise called "taking
inventory." English, math, and history teachers have an
easy time of this; but it's a Gargantuan headache for science,
music, and shop teachers, who are responsible for equipment
worth many thousands of dollars, and who must account
for every gram of mercury, every music rack, and every lug

wrench. Even an English teacher with a room full of paper-
back books will find inventory a formidable affair if he
procrastinates until the day before the deadline.

Be sure to arrange your lesson plans during the last week
of school so that the only teaching resource you or the students will need will be a mimeographed study outline. You'll
be reviewing for examinations anyway, won't you?

Ask for enough extra inventory forms to allow for working
copies. There will be erasures, cross-outs, and write-ins.
Don't type up your official copy until you are positive you
have included everything. Also, be sure to make a carbon
copy for yourself. You will use it in the fall to be sure nothing
has walked out of your classroom while you were gone over
the summer (highly likely if a summer school class has been
conducted in your room).

If you have dependable students who can give you free
time after school to help with your inventory, use them.
Spot-check their work to be sure you're getting accurate
counts.

Custodial Service

If the school is large, there will be a form for reporting to
the head custodian when a light bulb needs replacing or a
desk has been damaged. In most schools, you simply leave
a note in his box, tape a note on his door, or tell him when
you see him.

Supplies

You will probably fill out a form requesting the necessary
paper and other supplies to run your classroom. Ask for all
you need in September and, with luck, you won't need to
replenish your stocks until spring. Be sure to include:

1 box standard paper clips
½ box extra-large paper clips
1 box chalk (2 for math teachers)
1 chalkboard eraser for every ten running feet of board
   space around your room

1 box thumbtacks

25 spirit duplicating masters (more if you can get them)

1 dozen lead pencils

3 red grading pens, if available (You can get red grading pencils at school, but the points go dull quickly and pencil marks are easy for students to erase. Red felt-tip or ballpoint pens are better, but you may have to buy them yourself.)

1 ruler

1 stapler and box of staples to fit it

1 handful of rubber bands, assorted sizes

1 roll narrow masking tape

3 scratch pads

1 ream lined binder paper

1 ream spirit duplicator paper (more if you can get it)

Your supply clerk, usually a secretary in the office, may prefer to assemble these items for you at her convenience and have them delivered to your classroom later.

Classroom Forms

Paradoxically enough, less paper is required to exchange information about the curriculum than anything else. You may wish to develop certain forms for use with your own students so they can report data to you. Laboratory experiment forms, supplementary reading reports, physical fitness logs, and the like may prove useful in your classroom. You will work these out to suit your individual teaching requirements.

Curriculum and Textbook Evaluation

Your professional opinion may be solicited by questionnaire once or twice a year by the district's curriculum committee, or your evaluation of a proposed new textbook may be requested through a rating sheet once every five years. As a new teacher, you will feel yourself at a loss in filling out these reports; but you shouldn't use your lack of experience as an excuse for ducking your professional duty. Ask your department head or another experienced teacher if you may sit in with him when he fills out his form. Ask questions: "Why do you think this is good and that bad?" Next year, you will be able to make your own judgments more intelligently.

By all means, respond in some way to requests for your opinion, even if it's only to state that you have none. And once having responded in this way, please have the grace to abide by decisions made by the majority of your more experienced colleagues. The bane of the school is the teacher who has no opinion when asked, but later crabs about what everyone else decided to do.

Teacher Rating Sheets

Your school district will expect you to participate in the decision-making process, and your reluctance to assume your fair share of this responsibility will be reflected in other reports—not reports that are made *by* you, but reports that are made *about* you.

You realize, of course, that the district will keep records about you and your professional development as a basis for deciding whether or not to promote you to tenure status later on. There will be a rating sheet on which the principal, your department head, or a supervisor will judge you (you may be asked to evaluate yourself, too, for that matter) as excellent, superior, standard, poor, or unacceptable on a list of factors. These factors will include: teaching results, teaching methods, teacher-pupil relationships and classroom control, teacher-parent relationships, potentiality for successful teaching, professional ethics and basic attitudes toward the teaching profession, physical and mental fitness, attitude toward self-improvement, value to school outside of classroom, professional preparation, and appearance.

District policies vary when it comes to sharing the results of such ratings with the teachers themselves. Ask your department head about the practice in your school.

four

The Human Dimension

You'll build stronger relationships with your adolescent students, and build them more quickly, if you remember a basic fact about them: They're nervous. According to the University of Michigan Survey Research Center, juveniles are the age group that wins top honors in the worry department. No matter how insecure you may feel that first day of school, be assured the students seated before you are more insecure still. Apprehensive as they are about what you will think of them, they are even more apprehensive about what their fellow students are thinking about them.

Although the teen-ager by himself is as defenseless as a turtle without a shell, the teen-ager in a group is something else. Among his own kind, he has his guard up. He is the perpetual image builder, the full-time candidate in a popularity contest that is never finally won or lost. The pressure is murderous. Small wonder he is jittery and trigger-happy. The teacher's problem is to soothe and support him.

Play Fair

"Be fair, be friendly, be firm," is a well-worn educational aphorism with a millennium's worth of good left in it yet. Being fair demands several things. For one, it requires that you conduct your class for the instructional benefit of all your students, not just for the charming or noisy few. For another, it means enforcing rules with equal vigor for all. Class morale sinks to its lowest level in groups where penalties are generously imposed on some students but are nonexistent for others.

Being fair requires working out compromises that are acceptable to everyone. Conflicts will develop between you and your students, or between groups of students themselves, regarding classroom procedures. To resolve the inevitable impasses that will come about, draw lots, take turns, or trade one advantage for another.

Being fair implies the exercise of mature judgment. Before the gym instructor condemns his classes to an outdoor swimming lesson in sixty-degree weather, he should ask himself if he would relish a brisk plunge himself. More to the point, would he want his own son to take a swimming lesson under such conditions?

The Approach Approach

Americans are pumping many millions of dollars into education. We are buying new books, films, overhead projectors, computers, and language laboratories. We are trying the cross-cultural approach, the team teaching approach, the nongraded approach, and the systems approach. At length, after we have tried all these novelties and found to our surprise that nothing has really changed very much, our disillusionment may be raised to such a pitch of frenzy that we may try an approach so far out it borders on heresy. We may try befriending the students.

Yes, Virginia, there is a panacea. When you approach your students in a spirit of genuine friendship, 90 per cent of your teaching troubles evaporate. Where the young student is concerned, his motivation is a direct outgrowth of the motivation of the adults around him. If his teachers care enough about his future welfare to want him to learn, he will learn.

Simple friendship is one of the cheapest commodities to be found anywhere; and for the teacher, there can be no wiser investment. When you remember your students' names and speak to them in the hall, they will listen to you in class and try harder to remember what you said. When you remember to ask the girl in the senior play how rehearsals are coming along, she will straighten your books for you and keep your classroom neat. When you attend the game on a rainy night to root for the boy who's afraid he might be kicked off the team, he will do the homework you assign.

The friendly teacher projects optimism and good will. For the average adolescent, as anxiety-ridden as a laboratory mouse on an electric grid, the teacher's friendly manner is a classroom necessity if his self-consciousness is to be overcome and a constructive learning atmosphere maintained. Make no mistake about it, it is the quality of the relationships between the teachers and the students that ultimately determines whether a school is any good or not.

Be Firm

In the spring of my first year of teaching, Albert, age ten, asked me if I planned to promote him to fifth grade. When I told him he'd pass, even his freckles flushed with pleasure.

"Thank goodness fer that!" he chirped. "Pa would whup
the daylights outa me if I flunked agin."

"Oh, Albert, what a thing to say! You know your father
doesn't beat you!"

"Sure, he does! He whups all us kids if we needs it. Didn't
your pa whup you when you was little?"

"Well, no . . . I can't remember . . . ."

Pity softened Albert's eyes, and he tried to cheer me up.
"Maybe he didn't care as much about you 'cause you was
a girl," he said hopefully.

Seeing that this comment landed wide of the mark, he
whispered gently, "You didn't turn out too bad, though.
Don't you worry. It didn't hurt you none."

This was my first encounter with such an amazing attitude.
I was so overcome, I went home that same afternoon and
gave my own two youngsters a couple of swats apiece to
reassure them that I loved them!

In the years since, I've taught close to two thousand young
people of various ages. Never once have I experienced anything that would cast doubt on the validity of Albert's
philosophy of discipline. On the contrary, there have been
hundreds of experiences that showed me he was right. Even
young people who claimed to feel the opposite proved themselves liars by their all-too-transparent actions. When I
demanded, sometimes harshly, that they fulfill their obligations, they reacted toward me with affection. But if I let
them slide by, they equated permissiveness with indifference
(or laziness) and reacted with hostility and contempt.

Teen-age riots aren't caused by too many rules, but by too
few. The teacher who plans to buy teen-age approbation by
selling them "freedom" is in for a surprise. Most of today's
teen-agers have had "freedom" up to here, and long for
consistent enforcement of sound disciplinary policies.

Uses, Misuses, and Obligations of Power

Even though there may be an occasional Friday afternoon
when the issue is in doubt, by and large, the student in the

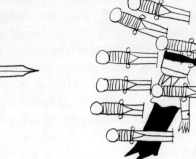

classroom is at the mercy of the teacher. State law and social custom traditionally vest as much authority in the school and the people who staff it as in the parent himself, and the student has almost as little power to change one as the other. If a student dislikes you or your class, scheduling limitations and graduation requirements often prevent his doing anything about it. If it's the entire school he doesn't like, his family must move to a new address to enable him to enroll in a different one—a costly process.

The teacher, therefore, has a moral obligation to his young captive audience. Obviously, he must teach them. That's what he's there for. He must not allow class session after class session to slip by as he maunders, gambols, harangues, or works crossword puzzles when he should be teaching. He should not use students and class time to take care of his personal affairs. He should not allow his class to become a perpetual kangaroo court devoted exclusively to the disposition of disciplinary problems.

Occasionally, one runs across teachers who sincerely feel that there is (or should be) no greater moral responsibility involved in conducting classes in a public school than there is in operating a bulldozer on a construction job. They argue that if a teacher wants to take a moonlighting job collecting protection money from prostitutes, this is his business and the school has no right to interfere. This kind of social astigmatism is hard to fathom. Teachers, like the clergy, must maintain higher standards of behavior than bulldozer operators. Whereas a bulldozer operator doesn't influence anything but dirt, teachers and the clergy influence large numbers of impressionable young people. And if teachers and the clergy don't maintain the moral standards of the community, who will? This may or may not be social justice, but's it's a social fact of life. Morally rotten teachers turn out morally rotten citizens. The teacher candidate who objects to this particular monkey on his back will do his nation a favor if he offers his services elsewhere.

The teacher must be a fit model for his students to emulate, for emulate him they will. They are far more likely to do as he does than they are to do as he says. ("Mrs. Ames doesn't pay any attention to school rules, why should I?" "Sure, I smoke. So do half the faculty members." "Mr. Smith passed out under the table at a nightclub last Saturday night; why shouldn't I take a drink or two?")

Keeping Peace with Parents

It's ironic that, stuck as we are smack in the middle of the "affluent society," the things that *really* improve the schools can't be bought with money at all. They can only be bought with human effort and imagination. Sound home-school relationships do more to insure the success of a school's educational effort than a faculty of Ph.D.'s. You should take advantage of opportunities to get to know the parents of your students. Let them know you care about the welfare of their children.

It's a terrible mistake to criticize any child's parents, ever. Once you get to know your students well, they will tell you the most outrageous things about their life at home. ("Dad beats up the old lady every week end." "Ma's boy friend comes to see her after I leave for school.") How much of it can you believe? We-ll-ll, *maybe* about 25 per cent—about as much as parents should believe of the tales kids bring home with them from school.

Why do kids tell these tales? For the same reason they tell the school tales at home. They get angry at the teacher for some reason or other and use this method to retaliate, or perhaps they're bored and want to stir up a little excitement. At any rate, don't be conned into reacting with comments like, "Your nasty, mean father! He should be horsewhipped for doing such a thing," etc. Next week, when the kid is no longer angry at his father, he will remember your condemnation. You denounced *his father*! He won't forget it, and it will take him a long time to forgive you. This situation is in the same league with the guy who bellyaches about his wife. If you agree with him that the woman is a tramp, you're a goner!

There will be one case in a hundred where you suspect the youngster is understating, not overstating, his difficulties at home, and authorities really should be notified. Perhaps he comes to school with some suspicious bruises. If in doubt, talk to the student's counselor. You may find the student has a notorious reputation for tall tales, or you may find there has been a long history of child abuse, arrests of the parents, foster homes, and so on.

No matter what the circumstances, sympathize with the student as you see fit, but *do not* criticize the parent. Blood is thicker than water to the power of about ten. No cause whatever is served by joining with a child against his parents.

The Parent Interview

Don't expect all parents to be easy to get along with, any more than all your fellow teachers or all the students in your classes will be easy to get along with. At one time or another, you will have to ask a parent to come to school to discuss problems, usually disciplinary, about a son or daughter. The first year, you should include an administrator or a counselor at such conferences. Why? Because the parent might chew you to ribbons. In nearly every state there are laws to protect the teacher from verbal and physical abuse from parents; but if there is no witness, what recourse have you?

Prepare carefully for parent interviews. Write down the

topics you want to discuss. Be sure you have documentation
—the student's papers, the desk he carved up, your gradebook, whatever is relevant. Invite both parents, even though
only the mother is likely to come. Set the time of the conference during the school day and arrange to be free at that
time. From the counselor, obtain the student's cumulative
folder and look it over. You should know when similar
conferences have been called before, and why.

The day before the conference, make arrangements for the
student to be present at the interview. You may have to have
him released from class. If the meeting is before or after
school, be sure the parent understands that the student is
expected to be present.

Arrive at the conference room a few minutes early. Check
to see that everything you need is there. Greet the parent,
invite everybody to sit down, and come to the point immediately.

Some mothers will be more co-operative than others, even
though at first they may not seem to be co-operative at all.
For example, there is the mother who will insist "my son
never lies." Hear her out. When she runs down, present your
documented evidence. She will eventually see her boy in a
different light, and there may be a few tears when she discovers he is normal after all and has told his "first" lie. She
arrives at the conference on the defensive and leaves deflated
and let down. You will see an improvement in the behavior
of the son.

Another conference that generally turns out well, although while it's going on you'll think it won't, is the one with the mother who drops names. She is a Very Important Person. She knows the superintendent of the district and all the officers of the P.T.A. (never serves as officer herself, only knows those who do). She knows the county superintendent and the state superintendent of education. She makes it clear to you that because of her many community responsibilities, she shouldn't be bothered with such matters as petty disciplinary problems at school. Even supposing there has been a problem at all with her son, which she doubts, why can't the school handle these situations in its own way without bothering her? She refuses to admit there is anything to worry about. After some time passes in this fashion, she suddenly collapses, perhaps after pointedly glancing at her watch ("Oh dear! Only ten minutes to get to my next meeting!"), and sighs, "All right, what do you want?" When told, she agrees to attend to it, usually means it, and leaves thinking she has won still another battle because she knew the right people.

Occasionally you'll have a mother-father conference where the mother does all the talking. ("Isn't that right, John?" "Didn't we agree, John, that . . . ." "Don't pay any attention to John; he hasn't adjusted to the current trends.") John gets the blame for the student's failures, and mother takes the credit for his virtues. The best thing to do in this case, after you have silently awarded John an ample portion of unsolicited pity, is to listen. She will eventually admit her child has done wrong, and you can be sure that child will never be in trouble again. (But poor John!)

Curiously, you can expect almost no result at all from the most co-operative mother of the lot. This lady will have dressed carefully for her school visit. She will tell you what a fine job the school is doing. ("I wouldn't be a teacher for anything! You people are so noble, so dedicated. You're overworked and underpaid. Yes, I know my son did wrong, and I'm grateful to you for arranging this conference so we could talk about it. Yes, indeed, I *certainly will* lay down the law to Billy. He mustn't be allowed to get by with such things. Thank you so much for letting me know about this problem.") Gush. Goo. Smiles. "Bye, now." Smiles. She has done her duty and eaten humble pie with the school people to buy them off. She feels her obligation has been discharged, and that's the end of it. Her child sits, smiling contentedly, through the conference, secure in the knowledge that, except for the joke he will share with Mom after they get home, nothing, absolutely nothing, will change. Mark this kid's folder for big trouble later.

A first cousin of the lady above is the "wild oats" mother. ("You were young once yourself, weren't you?") She is pleasant to talk to and quick to apologize for her child's destructive actions and to confess that she is probably responsible; she has over-reacted to her own strict upbringing, she will tell you. Regardless of what she says, she inwardly admires and envies her child's authority-challenging behavior. Her only true regret is that he was caught. Some good might be salvaged from this conference by getting the father in on the problem, but it will only be a temporary stopgap. This kid, like the one with the gushy mother, is a loser.

Far and away the most unpleasant of any parent conference you'll have will be the one with the ex-schoolteacher. Now it shouldn't come as a surprise to you that male and female school personnel reproduce like everybody else and have children who go to school. Sometimes the children get into trouble. *Employed* teachers, counselors, and administrators are usually goaded by pride and professional responsibility to attend to difficulties that crop up with teachers of their own children. The mother or father who is an *ex-*schoolteacher is something else again. You may wonder about the "ex." Was this person fired? Probably. If so, you are in the direct line of fire to catch a blast of acrimony having little to do with the immediate problem. Brace yourself. In terms of influencing the student's future behavior, the conference need not be a waste of time at all. His vituperative parent will embarrass him so painfully that he won't risk a repeat performance and will probably stay out of trouble for good. Try to understand this youngster. Be especially cautious about advising him in any manner or speaking out about his parents. Then forget the conference, if possible.

How To Win Friends in the Faculty Lounge

Although most new teachers are a joy to have on the faculty, there is the occasional maniac everyone wishes would drop dead. It will be his classes that will tie up the auditorium or the cafeteria for days and throw the schedule out of kilter. It will be his homeroom students who will erupt like scorched ants to embark on projects of such scope as to put UNESCO to shame, and so poorly planned as to make the principal writhe. He will be the one to upset precedents of years' standing in an attempt to "get some life" into the teachers' organization. He will be the one who will clobber the departmental meeting agenda as he enthusiastically explains for forty-five minutes how he and his friends did it last year in Methods 263. In short, this new teacher will be the one whose nimbus of excessive zeal will demobilize anyone within a radius of sixty yards. Anyone, that is, too slow on his feet to get out of the way.

"What a pity there isn't a way to bottle that energy and save it for next year when he'll have more sense," a twenty-year teacher once commented, thereby summing up the situation.

A school's new and recently-trained teachers are a valuable resource. You will receive a sincere welcome in your new school; have no qualms on that score. If, in addition, you come prepared to learn the rudiments of day-to-day school life *before* you begin brandishing your reformer's pennant, the older teachers will do their best to shelter you from the harsh realities of your first year; they will also listen to what you have to say the second year, when they are more confident you know what you're talking about.

So do, please, try to temper your enthusiasm. Do a few things well, rather than many things badly. Do more listening than talking, more observing than showing off. Education has waited for you since the beginning of time; it can wait a few months longer until you are broken to harness.

The Teacher and His Professional Organization

The cause of education is more ably served when new teachers enter their first teaching positions with a backlog of high school and college experience in clubs and politics. They already will have discovered, for example, that the democratic process means the majority rules. The minority, having tried but failed to win a majority of favorable votes, must go along with the final decision, no matter how nefariously wrong they may feel that decision to be, and hope for better luck next time. This is the same plan we adopted for running our country some two hundred years ago, and, all things considered, it has worked out fairly well.

Sometimes new teachers don't understand the rules of the game very well. Especially in geographic areas where teacher turnover is high, politically naïve personnel coming into a teacher's organization can turn the thing into a shambles

before the president can say, "It has been moved and seconded." Without mentioning their intention to anyone, they may petition the school board to discontinue a medical insurance plan it took a teachers' committee five years to negotiate. It isn't always ignorance that makes people do this. Sometimes a group of teachers know the rules as well as the next person, but choose to ignore them because they haven't the imagination to get things done any other way. A group of unauthorized rebels may attend the school board meeting to insist that Washington's birthday be declared a school holiday, when only the year before last, by action of the entire teachers' group, Washington's birthday was sacrificed for a longer Easter vacation.

Regardless of their motives, renegade teachers are bad news for everybody. They place administrators and the school board in embarrassing dilemmas. When they make headlines in the newspapers, which they sometimes do, they give the community's teachers a black eye and make pay raises and bond issues more difficult to achieve. Among their more experienced colleagues, whose efforts they undermine, they inspire the same kind of murderous hatred the loyal union member feels for the scab.

By all means, join a teachers' organization. But having joined, do what you can to make it more significant as a force for good in the life of your community. In a few short years, you younger teachers will be called upon to assume leadership roles. It will be a more gratifying task if you inherit an organization you're proud of.

Epilogue

Sometime during your first year in the classroom, you may suddenly come awake with a start and gaze about you at the noisy kaleidoscope of bells, slips of paper, books, and teeming humanity. As though seeing it all for the first time, you will ask yourself, "What are all these people *doing* here?"

Well, all those people are there to learn. Your job is to see that information from your head, the books, the films, the charts, the maps, and the shop manuals ends up in the heads of those kids sitting at the desk in your classroom. This is the point of the game. This is the *only* point of the game.

All of us in education need a harder nose and a clearer eye in the way we approach our jobs. Are we really teaching? How do we know? At least once in his lifetime, every teacher in the land should give a final exam at the beginning of the school year as well as at the end. In this way, the net gain in learning a teacher has brought about in his students can be measured. Such an experiment isn't recommended as standard practice for the fainthearted or the easily threatened. The first time I tried it, years ago, I crawled under a rock and didn't come out for two weeks. New teachers certainly shouldn't try anything of this kind until they've had a few years of experience. If they did, they'd quit in despair—and we can't spare them.

What the new teacher can do is develop objectivity about his work in the classroom. If the entire class flunked the test, was it because the students were lazy and didn't learn? Was it because the test was poorly constructed? Was it because the material wasn't taught very well? Blaming student interest without exploring the possibility of other inadequacies is the amateur's way out, yet secondary school people, year after year, continue to make grave mistakes in this direction.

The bitter truth is that we teach far less than we think we do. In our classrooms, we pay attention to peripheral matters that we assume are improving either the quantity or the quality of the educational end product, but we seldom follow up in a methodical way to find out if they actually have or not. The new teacher should avoid this trap.

Your first year of teaching in your own classroom will be more difficult than your last year as a college student. There'll be no supervising teacher, professor, or advisor there for the express purpose of helping you. True, you will be surrounded by people who will be glad to answer your questions or assist you as much as they can, but in order to help you, these people will be sacrificing time they might be devoting to their own responsibilities.

You will find yourself making your own decisions; and, because you will be new at your job, not all of these decisions will be wise. You must expect this. As your obligations mount, you will have many moments when you feel power-less and confused. When faced with fifteen tasks that must be attended to, you'll find you must set up priorities. Which chores must be done immediately and carefully? Which can wait until tomorrow or next week? Which can be given a lick and a promise? Are there any that can be forgotten about altogether? First things first, yes; but what divining rod does one use to decide what comes first?

The kids. Teach the kids first, and everything else will fall into place.

Index